Good Country

_____ *THIS RIVER* _____
____ *THE MUSKOKA* ____
GARY LONG

THIS RIVER
THE MUSKOKA

GARY LONG

THE BOSTON MILLS PRESS

Canadian Cataloguing in Publication Data

Long, Gary
   This river the Muskoka

  Bibliography: p.
  Includes index.
  ISBN 1-55046-012-9

  1. Muskoka River (Ont.) · History.   I. Title.

  FC3095.M93L66 1989   971.3'16   C89-094442-3
  F1059.M93L66 1989

All photographs by author unless otherwise acknowledged.

Published by:
THE BOSTON MILLS PRESS
132 Main Street
Erin, Ontario N0B 1T0
(519) 833-2407
FAX: 833-2195

American Association
for State and Local History
Award of Merit

Winners of the
Heritage Canada
Communications Award

Design by John Denison
Cover design by Gill Stead
Typography by Lexigraf, Tottenham
Printed by Ampersand, Guelph

The publisher wishes to acknowledge the encouragement
and the financial assistance of The Canada Council, the
Ontario Arts Council and the Office of the Secretary of State.

TABLE OF CONTENTS

I dedicate this book to my parents, Marilyn and George Long of Bracebridge, who instilled in me a love and respect for the natural environment, and encouraged me in every way to pursue my interests.

FOREWORD

The Muskoka River has long been a hobby of mine. For years I've explored its nooks and crannies, talked to dozens of people who knew more about it than I did, and searched libraries and archives for more clues about its past. Gradually I realized that this interesting waterway has been possibly the most significant influence on the settlement and development of Muskoka District.

In 1986 I gathered the results of my research into a 22-part series for the *Muskoka Sun* newspaper. That series, titled "This River the Muskoka," was quite well received, I'm happy to say, and a number of individuals encouraged me to have it published as a book.

And so, this volume is the result. Although I've incorporated in it much of the material from the newspaper series, I've extensively re-organized and rewritten the text, and added new information and more historical photographs.

In this book, as in the newspaper series, I haven't attempted to cover all aspects of the Muskoka River; the emphasis is on the historical role of the waterway and its fascinating natural history. Even so, I've only been able to include a fraction of all the information available. For further reading you'll find many useful publications listed in the bibliography at the end.

As a geographer, I put a lot of stock in maps, and thus I've put a lot of maps in this book to complement the written word and photos. You'll find it helpful to refer to five maps in particular as you read along: two in Chapter 2 which provide an overview of the whole Muskoka River system and its environs; and three more at the end of Chapter 11 that cover the watershed in greater detail. Since this is not a guidebook, you should consult readily available topographic or district maps for roads and other details.

I would like to thank the Ontario Arts Council for financial assistance in the preparation of this book, and of course all those individuals who knowingly or unknowingly helped me learn more about this river the Muskoka.

Gary Long,
Huntsville, 1989.

SANDY GRAY'S CHUTE, *Musquash River. The largest untamed falls remaining on the Musquash thunders into the east end of rock-rimmed, pine-fringed Flatrock Lake. Log-driver Sandy Gray lost his life here over 120 years ago.*

CHAPTER 1

This River the Muskoka: Lifestream of the District

What comes to mind when you think of Muskoka? Certainly one of the most compelling images must be the rugged beauty of the landscape: the ancient rock, the wooded hills, the myriad of lakes and streams sparkling across the southern fringe of the Canadian Shield.

Muskoka has been viewed in many ways over the years: as a rich habitat for the fur-bearing animals that provided a livelihood for trappers and fur traders; as a land rich in timber for the lumber companies and hemlock bark for the tanneries; as a new frontier for hundreds of hopeful settlers; and as a vacation-land for untold thousands from the cities to the south.

Yet through these diverse activities and attractions there runs a common thread: the waterways. If I had to choose that component of Muskoka's natural heritage which has played the biggest role in the economy and life of the district, I would have to choose the river — the Muskoka River.

Over the years other resources — the fur-bearing animals, the pockets of tillable soil, the forests of pine, hemlock and hardwoods — have briefly dominated the economy, and today still play lesser though not unimportant roles. But the lakes and streams that make up the Muskoka River system have always been vital to the district. Indeed, they often made possible the utilization of the region's other resources.

The Muskoka River actually starts just east of Muskoka, up in the lofty hills and lakes of Algonquin Provincial Park, but for most of its length it winds across the district and down to the wind-swept shores of Georgian Bay. Through its scores of tributaries and hundreds of lakes, it drains all but the southern fringes of Muskoka. The river is, in essence, the physical heart and lifestream of the district.

It is also its scenic heart. Thundering waterfalls and splashing rapids, smooth waters gliding dark and silent through the forested hills, crystal lakes with majestic pines soaring on rocky promontories — these all contribute immeasurably to Muskoka's renowned beauty. The river's scenic wealth, combined with the tremendous recreational opportunities provided by its lakes and streams, has made Muskoka a mecca for vacationers since the earliest days of settlement. The resort, tourism and cottage industry took over as a mainstay of the Muskoka economy after agriculture and lumbering faltered.

Tourism in Muskoka today doesn't depend totally on the river. In recent years the mushrooming popularity of such winter activities as cross-country skiing and snowmobiling has made the district a year-round playground. Nonetheless, it is safe to say that the streams, and particularly the lakes, still contribute most to the vital tourism sector of the economy.

The Muskoka River has proved its worth in many other

ways, too. Back when virgin wilderness covered all of Muskoka, the lakes and streams served as canoe routes for Indian hunters and trappers, and later for fur traders, explorers and surveyors. When the settlement of Muskoka officially began in 1859, the waterways continued their vital transportation role. Roads in the early pioneer days, little more than rutted trails, were an arduous way of getting about. The canoe continued as an important mode of transport for many early settlers.

However, when we look at the river system from a transportation standpoint, the introduction of the steamboat stands out as the event that revolutionized the movement of passengers, freight and raw materials in the district. Although numerous waterfalls rendered the rivers unnavigable for any great distance, a few relatively minor navigation improvements — locks, short canals and dredging — made it possible for steamboats to ply the big inland lake chains in the central part of the Muskoka watershed. Beginning in 1866 and continuing for several decades, the steamers maintained a dominant role in the Muskoka transportation system.

The steamers did much to encourage settlement and industry by providing fast, reliable access to some 20 townships and dozens of communities. Perhaps they made their biggest contribution by helping to open up the lakes to the resort and tourism industry. As time went on, private motorboats, automobiles and an improved road network rendered the steamers increasingly redundant; nonetheless, some of them continued to serve as cruise boats until as late as 1958. After a complete overhaul, the last survivor of the big steamboats, the *Segwun*, began to ply the familiar waters of the Muskoka Lakes again in 1981, much to the delight of everyone captivated by her quiet, stately charm.

As a transportation route the Muskoka River played a central role in the lumbering industry in Muskoka. For over 80 years lumbermen used it as a water highway to float millions of logs out of the hills and down to the sawmills. In the days before trucks became available, there was often no other way to move large quantities of timber long distances.

Up until the reserves of pine in the Muskoka watershed were virtually logged out early this century, lumbering was the leading industry in Muskoka. Without the river it could never have gained prominence at the time it did, a time when settlers struggling to eke out a living from the thin soils of the Canadian Shield desperately needed an additional source of income. Lumbering continues today in Muskoka, but on a smaller scale based on the hardwoods rather than on the pine. The truck has replaced the river as the means of transporting the logs to the sawmills.

The numerous waterfalls along the Muskoka River and its tributaries proved a great hindrance to driving logs. In addition they created obstacles to navigation that could not have been overcome without great difficulty. On the other hand, many of these waterfalls greatly benefited the pioneers by providing a readily harnessed source of energy for small frontier sawmills and grist mills, Muskoka's first industrial establishments.

Although the water-powered mills were soon superceded in overall economic importance by large steam-powered mills and factories, they played a vital role in early pioneer life. They saved many a settler from long, arduous days hand-sawing planks and greatly reduced the distances he had to trek carrying sacks of grain to be ground into flour.

In later years the water-power potential of Muskoka River waterfalls again rose to prominence, when it was harnessed to generate electricity at hydroelectric stations. For several decades these stations supplied virtually all of Muskoka's electricity and substantial amounts for areas to the south. Ten hydroelectric stations (11 if you include a small private installation) operate on the Muskoka River today. They produce enough electricity for about 12,000 homes.

Such have been the important and varied roles of the Muskoka River in shaping the settlement and development of Muskoka that it is easy to overlook the river itself as a natural element of the landscape. Rivers are fascinating. They constantly evolve, shaping the land by their erosion and deposition. As the terrestrial link in the great hydrologic cycle that circulates the waters of the planet through the land, seas and air, rivers represent one of the major dynamic forces that mould our world.

Although it is hardly a major stream by world, or even Ontario standards, the Muskoka River boasts a natural history as interesting as that of any larger stream. Like many Canadian rivers, the Muskoka is a child of the Ice Age, born just a few thousand years ago upon the retreat of the huge glaciers that overran much of the country. The characteristics and scenery of the river today still bear the imprint of glaciation. The waterfalls and many of the lakes we find so attractive, and the sand beaches enjoyed by thousands each summer, all owe their origins to the ice. The ice scraped and carved the ancient rock underneath, its meltwaters dumped billions of tonnes of sand, gravel, silt and clay in the valleys and in the margins of a huge post-glacial lake, Lake Algonquin, that once flooded much of Muskoka. The Muskoka River has been eroding into these deposits ever since.

The Muskoka River is so young — young in geologic terms — that it has not yet made much impact on the foundations of the land it drains, those very hard ancient rocks of the Canadian Shield. The topography created by this rock, sculptured by the ice and by pre-glacial ancestors of the Muskoka into forms dictated by the structure of the rock itself, determines the courses of the streams, the size and depth of the lakes, and the location and appearance of the waterfalls.

Inevitably, as the river continues its slow, inexorable work of erosion, it will shape the rock that has so far shaped it. That is the natural destiny of rivers. They evolve, changing the landscape, and in so doing, altering their own characteristics. The Muskoka River we see today is just a snapshot in its life. In the past it looked very different than it does now, and in the future, far beyond our lifetimes, it will bear no resemblance to its present state.

Flowing water, of course, is what makes a river. Its volume determines the size of the channel, its energy permits the erosion and transport of rock and soil, its abundance or scarcity, purity or contamination, affects the ways we can use our waterways. Geographic circumstances insure that the Muskoka River normally carries an abundance of water — an overabundance at times. On the other hand, during prolonged droughts it carries very little. Over the years numerous dams have been built on the river to regulate stream flows and lake levels to better serve a variety of needs.

Since the 1850s the story of the Muskoka River has been one of the intensive use of its desirable features and the elimination or circumvention of its obstacles, to fuel the economy of Muskoka District. Through the course of this book we'll look in greater detail at some of the ways the river has served the lumbermen, the settlers, the millers, steamboat operators, resort owners and electric utilities.

We'll follow in the wake of the men who first explored the river, discover how the lakes, streams and waterfalls got their names, and learn how a system evolved for the management of the river.

Recognizing the importance of the natural heritage of the river, for its own sake and for its influence on economic and cultural activities, we'll also touch on the natural history of the Muskoka River — the geology and evolution of its channels, lakes and waterfalls — and the factors that affect the flow of water through it.

I'm sure that in the end you'll agree that this river the Muskoka fully deserves its billing as the lifestream of Muskoka District.

CHAPTER 2

Untangling the Waterways: The Muskoka River from Source to Mouths

The Muskoka River is not a single stream bearing that name from one end to the other. It's made up of complex chains of lakes and channels whose waters converge only briefly as they cross Muskoka District, then take separate courses to Georgian Bay.

More than a century and a half ago explorers began using the name Muskoka to refer to a particular route through the network of waterways all the way from the source to the mouth. However, the Muskoka doesn't have one dominant source, nor does it have a single mouth, and each link in the chain possesses its own unique character. Over the years each has received its own name. Thus when we speak of the Muskoka River, we are really talking about the Muskoka River *system*.

The Muskoka River system is one of several rivers draining off the Algonquin Dome, a huge bulge of ancient rock (part of the Canadian Shield) stretching from Georgian Bay in the west to the Ottawa Valley in the east, and from Lake Nipissing south to the Kawartha Lakes. The various rivers flow outwards like spokes of a wheel down the slopes of the Dome to the surrounding valleys and lake basins.

The longer and larger of these rivers rise well up on the highest part of the Dome, on the Algonquin Highland. This lofty lake- and hill-strewn tableland occupies much of the central and southwestern parts of Algonquin Provincial Park.

This is where the Muskoka River begins; from this elevated perch it tumbles generally west-southwesterly across Muskoka District to Georgian Bay.

Although not mountainous by any means, the Algonquin Highland attains elevations not far short of being the highest in Ontario. The summits of several hills in the headwaters of the Muskoka River lie some 400 metres (1,312 feet) above Georgian Bay — 577 metres (1,893 feet) above sea level. From its principal and most distant source in these hills, the Muskoka flows 219 kilometres (136 miles) to Georgian Bay. That's the distance measured along the sinuosities of the channel.

The Muskoka starts out as tiny creeks splashing down hillsides into the headwater lakes, but along some parts of its lower reaches it attains an average width close to 60 metres (200 feet). By the average flow of water from its mouths the Muskoka ranks as the third-largest river draining the southern Ontario land mass.

The Muskoka River collects its water from a roughly rectangular watershed, or drainage basin, that measures 125 kilometres (78 miles) long and sprawls 5,110 square kilometres (1,973 square miles) up the western slope of the Algonquin Dome. That's a chunk of land only slightly smaller than the province of Prince Edward Island.

The Muskoka watershed encompasses the northern three

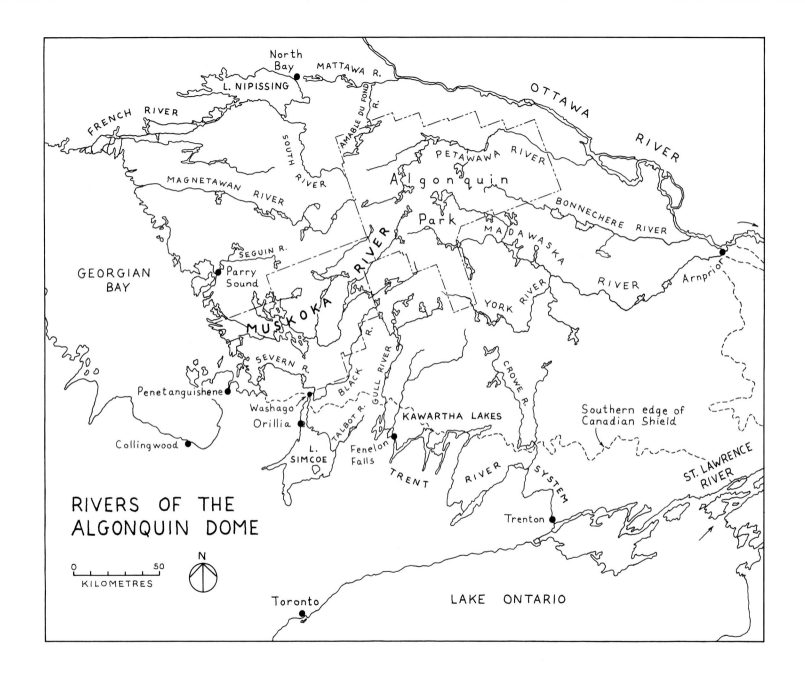

North
Bay
MATTAWA R.
L. NIPISSING
OTTAWA
FRENCH RIVER
SOUTH RIVER
AMABLE DU FOND R.
PETAWAWA RIVER
RIVER
MAGNETAWAN RIVER
Algonquin
BONNECHERE RIVER
SEGUIN R.
MADAWASKA
Park
GEORGIAN BAY
Parry Sound
MUSKOKA RIVER
YORK RIVER
RIVER
Arnprior
SEVERN R.
CROWE R.
BLACK R.
GULL RIVER
Penetanguishene
Washago
Orillia
TALBOT R.
KAWARTHA LAKES
Southern edge of
Canadian Shield
Collingwood
L. SIMCOE
Fenelon Falls
TRENT   RIVER   SYSTEM
ST. LAWRENCE RIVER

RIVERS OF THE
ALGONQUIN DOME

Trenton

0   50
KILOMETRES

N

Toronto
LAKE ONTARIO

quarters of Muskoka District, the southern fringe of Parry Sound District, and in the east, corners of Haliburton County and Algonquin Provincial Park. The lower quarter of Muskoka District drains south through the Black River and several smaller streams into the Severn River, which, after leaving Lake Couchiching (the northern arm of Lake Simcoe), forms part of the southern boundary of the district.

Typical of Canadian Shield terrain, the watershed of the Muskoka River is rough and hilly, cloaked with forests, strewn with lakes and closely underlain by ancient gneiss which is frequently exposed. The topography created by this underlying bedrock determines the courses of the Muskoka River and its tributaries.

In the eastern three quarters of the watershed the general arrangement of streams follows that of most river systems: a network of tributaries continually merging to form increasingly larger streams and ultimately the mainstream river, creating a pattern somewhat resembling the branches and trunk of a deciduous tree. Superimposed upon and often obscuring this pattern are the hundreds of lakes for which Muskoka is famous. Closer to Georgian Bay the normal converging pattern gives way to a diverging arrangement of distributaries — a not uncommon anomaly on the glaciated Shield. Distributaries are normally found only where rivers have built up deltas at their mouths.

The Muskoka River trunk stream, or mainstream, starts at Bracebridge from the confluence of its two largest branches, the North Muskoka and the South Muskoka (officially the North Branch and the South Branch of the Muskoka River). These two large streams, virtually identical in size, together drain the entire eastern two thirds of the Muskoka watershed.

The South Muskoka actually carries about six percent more water than the North Branch, technically making it the main tributary of the Muskoka. Early explorers considered it a continuation of the Muskoka mainstream, but only because it provided the best canoe route up to the height of land on the Algonquin Highland, and thence into the headwaters of the eastward-flowing Madawaska and Petawawa rivers. In practice you cannot tell by looking at the two rivers which is the larger.

Both the North and South branches have their principal headwaters among the rugged hills of the Algonquin Highland in western Algonquin Park. The South Muskoka begins up there as the Oxtongue River, gathering its water from long chains of lakes twisting through the high, rolling hills. Tea, Smoke, Canoe, Joe, and Burnt Island, to name just a few Highland lakes, are well known to thousands of Algonquin Park canoe trippers. Burnt Island Lake (or to be more precise, a small creek flowing into its northeastern extremity) is the true source of the South Muskoka and, by extension, of the Muskoka River system.

The waters of these headwater lakes all converge in Tea Lake, from which the Oxtongue emerges as a full fledged river. The Oxtongue then flows 48 kilometres (30 miles) southwesterly to the northern arm of Lake of Bays near Dwight. Along the way it plunges a whopping 103 metres (338 feet) — it literally falls off the edge of the Algonquin Highland. The lion's share of that descent is contributed by some spectacular waterfalls and treacherous rapids within a few kilometres above and below Oxtongue Lake. For the most part, however, the Oxtongue flows sedately, meandering along the sandy floor of its largely wilderness valley, murmuring often across gravel bars, occasionally spilling over ledges of rock to form scenic little chutes lost in the vast forests.

In addition to the Oxtongue, the South Muskoka has a second major tributary, the Hollow River, which drops into the eastern arm of Lake of Bays near Dorset. It runs just 11 kilometres (7 miles) from Hollow, or Kawagama, Lake just to the east, but it's fed by numerous wild creeks tumbling into Hollow Lake from the fringes of the Algonquin Highland to the north and east, and actually carries two thirds as much water as the Oxtongue. Hollow Lake is the focal point of the basin. Filled with clear, pristine waters, dotted with hulking central islands and ringed by undulating hills, it can be one of the most hauntingly beautiful bodies of water in the Muskoka River system.

Certainly the Hollow River itself is one of the prettiest streams around. Tucked into a fold in the hills east of Dorset, it sits on the doorstep of bustling cottage vacation land, yet for much of its length it surrounds you with a sense of distant wilderness and timeless beauty. Incredibly clear waters enhanced by a natural greenish tint find their way through a series of narrow little lakes and shady sun-dappled glens filled with splashing rapids and fragrant cedar and hemlock. Near the end of its journey, before it glides peacefully out into Lake of Bays, the Hollow boils down a long, rocky rapids and an impressive chute that account for over half of its 40-metre (131-foot) descent.

The second-largest and third-deepest lake in the Muskoka River watershed, Lake of Bays boasts scenery commensurate with its dimensions. Made up almost entirely of deep bays poking into the high green hills that rise all around, it possesses a character that is almost fjord-like in places. From its southwestern bay at Baysville, Lake of Bays spawns the South

Muskoka mainstream. The river follows a 46-kilometre (29-mile) J-shaped course south, then west, and briefly northward to its confluence with the North Muskoka at Bracebridge.

In reality a powerful stream descending a total of 90 metres (295 feet), the South Muskoka actually displays a rather subdued nature for most of its length. Its wide, deep and generally placid channel ambles between unobtrusive low hills or across sandy plains cloaked with pine, birch and maple forests. Only along its final few kilometres has it deeply entrenched itself in a valley. A series of attractive little chutes and rapids that occasionally interrupt the river along its upper reaches give way to higher and more powerful waterfalls further down, culminating in a thunderous descent over the greatest waterfall in central Ontario.

From the summits of the highest hills in the Oxtongue headwaters to the confluence with the North Muskoka, the South Muskoka falls some 352 metres (1,155 feet) over a distance of 150 kilometres (93 miles) and carries an average water flow of 28.5 cubic metres per second from a 1,740-square-kilometre (672-square-mile) watershed. The corresponding figures for the North Muskoka are remarkably similar. It descends the same amount from its highest source, and its length (131 kilometres, or 81 miles), average flow (26.8 cubic metres per second) and watershed area (1,580 square kilometres, or 610 square miles) are only slightly less.

Like the South Muskoka, the North Branch also begins under a different name, as the Big East River. The Big East headwaters rise on the rugged western rim of the Algonquin Highland, adjacent to those of the Oxtongue. Water pouring off the uninhabited hills quickly finds its way into several lively creeks that bubble down narrow valleys into a tiny

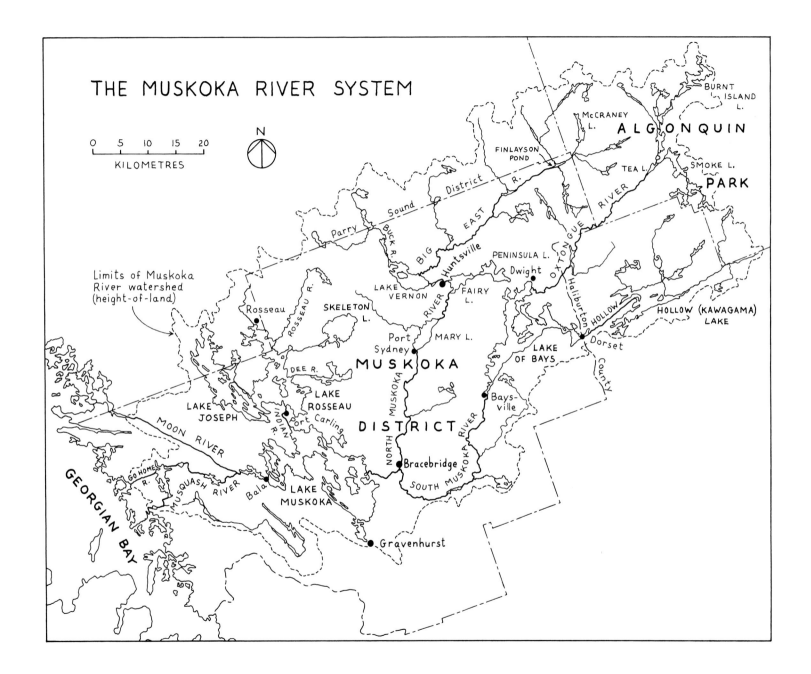

THE MUSKOKA RIVER SYSTEM

0 5 10 15 20
KILOMETRES

N

Limits of Muskoka
River watershed
(height-of-land)

ALGONQUIN

PARK

McCRANEY
L.

BURNT
ISLAND
L.

FINLAYSON
POND

SMOKE L.

TEA L.

Sound   District   R.

Parry

BUCK R.

BIG   EAST

RIVER

Huntsville

LAKE
VERNON

FAIRY
L.

PENINSULA L.

Dwight

OXTONGUE   RIVER

Haliburton

HOLLOW

Dorset

HOLLOW (KAWAGAMA)
LAKE

Rosseau

ROSSEAU R.

SKELETON
L.

Port
Sydney

MARY L.

MUSKOKA

LAKE
OF BAYS

County

DEE R.

LAKE
ROSSEAU

DISTRICT

Bays-
ville

LAKE
JOSEPH

INDIAN R.

Port Carling

NORTH   MUSKOKA   RIVER

MUSKOKA   RIVER

MOON RIVER

GO HOME
R.

MUSQUASH RIVER

Bala

LAKE
MUSKOKA

Bracebridge

SOUTH   MUSKOKA

GEORGIAN BAY

Gravenhurst

17

lake, Finlayson Pond, nestled in the far northeast corner of Muskoka District. Here, amid wooded hills that tower 150 metres (492 feet) above the water, the Big East becomes a river. Rushing headlong out of Finlayson Pond, it flows 50 kilometres (31 miles) across northern Muskoka to its mouth on Lake Vernon, just west of Huntsville.

Many of you probably know the Big East only as a shallow, lazy river winding tortuously along its broad, sandy valley near Huntsville, its summertime progress marked by gentle riffles alternating with deep black pools bordered by huge sandbars. Along the upper half of its course, however, the river gives a very different account of itself. The Big East makes virtually all of its 88-metre (289-foot) descent in the first 24 kilometres (15 miles) below Finlayson Pond. Rocky chutes and long, stony rapids (ten kilometres of them!) rush between quiet meandering reaches and the calm waters of ponds created by lumbermen in the late 1800s. Dense forests cascade down the steep valley sides to the silvery ribbon twisting back and forth in the bottom. The lonely grandeur of a mountain stream gushing out of the foothills pervades this wild upper reach of the Big East.

The North Muskoka doesn't have a second large tributary comparable to the Hollow River in the South Muskoka system. The unobtrusive and often forgotten Buck River, which falls into Lake Vernon from a chain of modest lakes and extensive marshes to the northwest, is only about a quarter the size of the Big East. Wandering through quiet woods and still marshes, it ends its journey with uncharacteristic violence as it tumbles down a set of scenic rapids and chutes.

The North Muskoka mainstream begins its 50-kilometre (31-mile) journey at the outlet of Lake Vernon. It curves briefly eastward through downtown Huntsville to Fairy Lake, then heads generally south down through Mary Lake and Port Sydney, and on to Bracebridge. A fourth major lake, Peninsula, lies just east of Fairy and is connected to it by a canal. The levels of Vernon, Fairy and Peninsula lakes are virtually the same — collectively, the three lakes are known as the Huntsville Lakes — while nearby Mary Lake is three metres (10 feet) lower.

In geographic extent the four big North Muskoka lakes equal Lake of Bays. They present picturesque expanses of ruffled blue waters cradled between steep, rolling hills — fantastic scenery in the autumn. Mary, Fairy and Vernon gain an extra element of ruggedness from islands that thrust rocky, pine-clad summits high above the water.

Like its southern sister, the North Muskoka flows generally wide, deep and leisurely; however, for its entire length it wends its way along the bottom of a deep valley that gives it a decidedly different character. The river drops markedly less than the South Muskoka — about 58 metres (190 feet) between Lake Vernon and Bracebridge — but the nature of its descent is the same. Scenic little chutes and rapids (mostly downstream from Mary Lake) are followed by large, powerful waterfalls as the river closes in on the end of its journey.

At Bracebridge a brief swirl of currents marks the confluence of the North and South Muskoka. The Muskoka River mainstream, born of this union, wanders uneventfully westward for just eight kilometres (5 miles) before emptying into Lake Muskoka. This huge island-filled expanse, by far the largest lake in the watershed, is the heart of the Muskoka River system and a true gathering place of waters. In addition to all the inflow from the east, it takes in that of the Indian River coming down through Port Carling from Lake Rosseau to the north.

Just six kilometres (3.7 miles) long and more closely resembling a strait than a river, the Indian nonetheless drains a watershed half the size that of the North Muskoka. A pair of huge lakes, Rosseau and Joseph, dominate the Indian River basin. Lake Joseph lies immediately west of Lake Rosseau and flows into it through the strait-like Joseph River and also through an artificial navigation cut at Port Sandfield. The two lakes stand at virtually the same elevation, less than a metre higher than Lake Muskoka. Lakes Rosseau and Joseph, together with Lake Muskoka, comprise the famous Muskoka Lakes.

The Muskoka Lakes possess a character all their own, quite unlike that of any others in the Muskoka watershed. Cradled not in deep valleys surrounded by lofty, rolling hills, they instead spread out across a vast landscape of scraped, almost desolate beauty — the Canadian Shield laid bare. Ancient rock abounds everywhere, sculptured into contorted shore-lines, protruding as hundreds of islands and peninsulas clad with sturdy oak and wind-blown pine. Breezy expanses of blue waters mingle with an incredible maze of rock-bound coves, bays and channels that seem to magnify the already impressive dimensions of these three lakes, which account for a third of all the lake surface in the Muskoka River system. For many people the Muskoka Lakes capture the very essence of Muskoka.

Four small rivers in the Muskoka Lakes region deserve mention because of their scenic and historical importance. Tumbling into Lake Rosseau from higher land to the east and northeast, these are the River Dee, rising in the pastoral valley of Three Mile Lake and then ambling across a landscape often reminiscent of a quiet English countryside; the delight-ful Skeleton, scampering off through the woods from the crystal-clear, bluff-rimmed waters of Skeleton Lake; the dark and languid Rosseau, occasionally awakening to sprint over scenic chutes; and finally the Shadow River, serene and shady along its lower reached, immortalized by famed Canadian poet Pauline Johnson.

The Muskoka Lakes are the last major lakes of the Mus-koka River system. From its westernmost extremity at Bala, Lake Muskoka overflows to start the river on the final dash down to Georgian Bay. This is the only place where practi-cally all of the water from the Muskoka watershed flows united. The union, however, is short-lived: less than six kilometres (3.7 miles) below Bala the river splits into two separate channels that take diverging courses to Georgian Bay. These are the Moon and Musquash rivers. The section between Bala and the fork — most of it really a lake — is officially considered part of the Moon River today. Some peo-ple call this stretch the Bala Reach.

Below the fork the Moon River trends almost straight northwest, flowing about 23 kilometres (14 miles) to the head of a chain of inlets and bays that lead out to the main body of Georgian Bay. Some consider this chain of bays to be a continuation of the Moon River. After branching off the Moon, the Musquash River spills somewhat haphazardly westward over a 31-kilometre (19-mile) course, passing through Go Home Lake shortly before entering Georgian Bay.

Go Home Lake also reaches Georgian Bay through a sec-ondary outlet called the Go Home River. Thus the Muskoka River system really has three outlets or mouths: the Moon, the Musquash and the Go Home. The Moon River was the natural main channel, but since 1938 an Ontario Hydro diver-sion has sent the bulk of the flow down the Musquash instead. The Moon functions primarily as a flood-water spillway now.

S. Penson. Del.

Only a small quantity of water from the Musquash seeps into Georgian Bay along the Go Home River.

All except 6 metres (20 feet) of the 48.5-metre (159-foot) descent of Muskoka River waters between Lake Muskoka and Georgian Bay occur downstream from the Moon · Musquash forks.

The Moon and Musquash rivers traverse a landscape of generally low relief, of seemingly endless waves of parallel rock ridges and intervening bogs where the forest struggles for existence and often fails. Few settlers tried to tame this forbidding terrain; it remains sparsely populated to this day. Much of the land along the Moon and Musquash is virtual wilderness.

The once powerful Moon carries hardly any water for most of the year. In the spring, though, it thunders to life and gives us a glimpse of its real personality. Wide and straight, it glides along with a sense of majesty and purpose between the steep, forested slopes of its confining ridges. Water, smooth and black, frequently crashes white and seething over roaring rapids and chutes that become larger and more spectacular as the river nears its mouth. Around the final two falls dry bald-rock slopes dotted with junipers push the forests away and pines stand defiantly on top of the ridges — a scene scraped and desolate and utterly captivating.

The Musquash River exists only by a fluke of geology and carries the great quantity of water that it does only by the design of man. Lacking a real valley of its own, it wanders this way and that, taking advantage of whatever grooves and gaps in the ridges it can find to make its way to Georgian Bay. Hydroelectric developments have drowned or silenced the falls and rapids along the upper reaches of the river. Further down, however, the inherently wild nature of the Musquash surfaces in force as the water roars over several chutes connecting a chain of rock-bound lakes fringed with pine and oak. In this starkly picturesque Go Home country adjacent to the Georgian Bay shores, the Muskoka River waters complete the last stage of their long journey that began up in the lush, rolling hills of the Algonquin Highland.

AMONG THE ISLANDS ON LAKE JOSEPH. *Calm waters lap rocky shores; silent woods of pine and oak heighten the solitude of the huge lake.*
· drawing by Seymour Penson in the *Guide Book and Atlas of Muskoka and Parry Sound Districts,* 1879

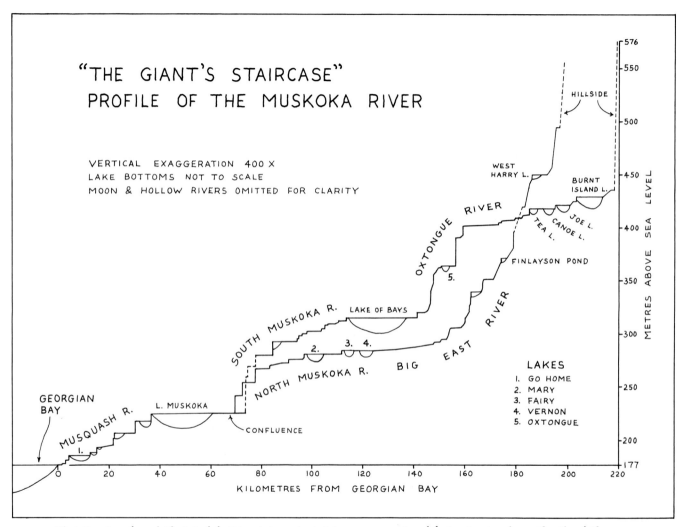

"THE GIANT'S STAIRCASE"
PROFILE OF THE MUSKOKA RIVER

VERTICAL EXAGGERATION 400 X
LAKE BOTTOMS NOT TO SCALE
MOON & HOLLOW RIVERS OMITTED FOR CLARITY

HILLSIDE

WEST HARRY L.
BURNT ISLAND L.
OXTONGUE RIVER
TEA L.
CANOE L.
JOE L.
FINLAYSON POND
5.
SOUTH MUSKOKA R.
LAKE OF BAYS
BIG EAST RIVER
2.
3. 4.
NORTH MUSKOKA R.

LAKES
1. GO HOME
2. MARY
3. FAIRY
4. VERNON
5. OXTONGUE

GEORGIAN BAY
MUSQUASH R.
L. MUSKOKA
CONFLUENCE
1.

METRES ABOVE SEA LEVEL

576
550
500
450
400
350
300
250
200
177

KILOMETRES FROM GEORGIAN BAY
0   20   40   60   80   100   120   140   160   180   200   220

Glaciation transformed the Muskoka River into a giant staircase — a series of basins stepping down the side of the Algonquin Dome. Waterfalls and rapids make up the vertical portions. Basins not occupied by lakes are filled with loose material deposited mainly by glacial meltwaters; nearly level stream channels cross these.

22

CHAPTER 3

Child of the Ice: The Birth and Evolution of the Muskoka River

The Muskoka River we know today looks very different than it did just a few thousand years ago. Indeed, 12,000 years ago the river didn't even exist. The processes that gave birth to the Muskoka River and shaped it into its present form add up to an exciting chapter in the river's history.

The story of the Muskoka River actually begins a billion years ago, long before advanced life evolved on Earth, in the era when geologic forces created the rock that underlies the watershed. This rock was formed during a lengthy period of upheaval when even older rock was subjected to enormous heat and pressure and intruded by molten magma deep in the Earth's crust. Transformed into metamorphic gneiss, it was thrust up into great mountain ranges.

Over the ages ancient streams and other forces of erosion slowly wore these mountains down until only their roots remained — the hills of the Algonquin Dome and adjacent southern parts of the Canadian Shield (Shield rock further north is much older). During one period huge seas covered the entire region. Layers of sediment deposited in the bottom of these seas were compressed into sedimentary rocks (such as limestone) which lay on top of the gneiss. After the seas receded, erosion removed most of the sedimentary formations to re-expose the older rock.

If we could go back in time just one million years we would find several rivers flowing down off the Algonquin Dome. At least one of them drained the land now drained by the Muskoka. That ancestral stream, however, bore little resemblance to the Muskoka we know: no dramatic waterfalls interrupted its course, no large lakes dotted the landscape. The river flowed swiftly at a relatively even grade down through wooded hills. In many places it no doubt followed valleys — indeed, helped dig valleys — now followed by streams of the Muskoka system, but in some areas it probably diverged from the present courses.

That period one million years ago is significant. That's when the climate began to cool and the Ice Age began, setting in motion the processes that would lead to the birth of the modern Muskoka River just a little over 11,000 years ago. In human terms 11,000 years seems a long time; on the geologic time scale it's just a blink of the eye. The Muskoka River is still an infant, a child of the ice.

Four times in the last million years great glaciers as much as 3,000 metres (2 miles) thick crept across most of Canada and into the northern United States. They ground over the Canadian Shield, the Algonquin Dome and the Muskoka watershed like giant excavators and bulldozers. They stripped off the forests and the soil and gouged into the bedrock underneath, scraping the hills, deepening the valleys and digging thousands of basins across the landscape.

Twenty thousand years ago, as the climate began to warm

up, the last of the glaciers began to melt northward. Over a period of a few hundred years, between 11,000 and 12,000 years ago, it uncovered the Muskoka watershed. During that time, then continuing for centuries afterwards, an incredible series of events marked the birth of the Muskoka River.

Meltwaters pouring from the receding glacier coursed out over the barren land, funneled into great spillways that roared down bedrock valleys into a huge post-glacial lake, Lake Algonquin, which briefly inundated the entire western half of the watershed. These meltwaters deposited billions of tonnes of gravel, sand, silt and clay that built up localized plains, clogged many valleys and extended deltas out into the margins of Lake Algonquin; nonetheless, glaciation left the greater portion of the Muskoka watershed with only a thin veneer of *drift* covering the rock beneath, much of it a jumbled mixture of material called *till* rather than the strati-fied deposits laid down by meltwaters.

In the higher, unflooded parts of the watershed, lakes filled many of the basins carved into the bedrock by the ice, waterfalls sprang into existence as new streams toppled from basin to basin between them. As Lake Algonquin receded, hundreds more lakes were stranded in those basins that hadn't been filled with drift. As new streams cut down into the glacial gravels, sands, silts and clays the rest of the chan-nels and waterfalls of the Muskoka River system gradually emerged and evolved. The river that before glaciation flowed as though running down a giant ramp now descended a huge stairway of lakes and placid channels interrupted by waterfalls and rapids.

Lake Algonquin occupied the basins of Georgian Bay, Lake Huron and Lake Michigan. At its maximum it stood at a level only about 7.5 metres (25 feet) above the present elevations of those water surfaces. The widespread flooding of the Muskoka watershed and other areas around it resulted because the great weight of the ice had depressed the land. The depth of this depression increased northward, where the ice had been thicker and had sat longer, and attained magni-tudes of several hundred metres.

When the ice melted, the land began to rebound, quickly at first, then at a decelerating pace. It continues to rise today at a rate that has been measured in centimetres per century. As a result of this *isostatic* uplift, the old Lake Algonquin shore can be traced across the Muskoka watershed at elevations high above Georgian Bay: over 110 metres (360 feet) above it in the south, rising to more than 160 metres (525 feet) above it in the north. In its time the lake was level, of course; the land to the north has simply rebounded further, having been depressed to a greater extent by the ice.

Due to the rocky nature of the land and the protection afforded by offshore islands, we don't find extensive Lake Algonquin beaches in the Muskoka watershed, as we do in other parts of Ontario, particularly to the south. Nonetheless, we can infer the approximate position of the shoreline from the location and elevation of deltas that formed where glacial meltwaters entered the lake, and by projecting the water plane to areas lacking such features. The presence of lacus-trine (lake bottom) clays and barren, wave-washed ridges also help delineate a large area that was inundated.

The Lake Algonquin shoreline ran roughly north-south through the Muskoka River watershed along a line generally just east of Highway 11. It was a rocky, irregular coast charac-terized by a maze of peninsulas, islands, inlets and channels — very much like the present east shore of Georgian Bay. A narrow bay extended some distance up the the South Mus-

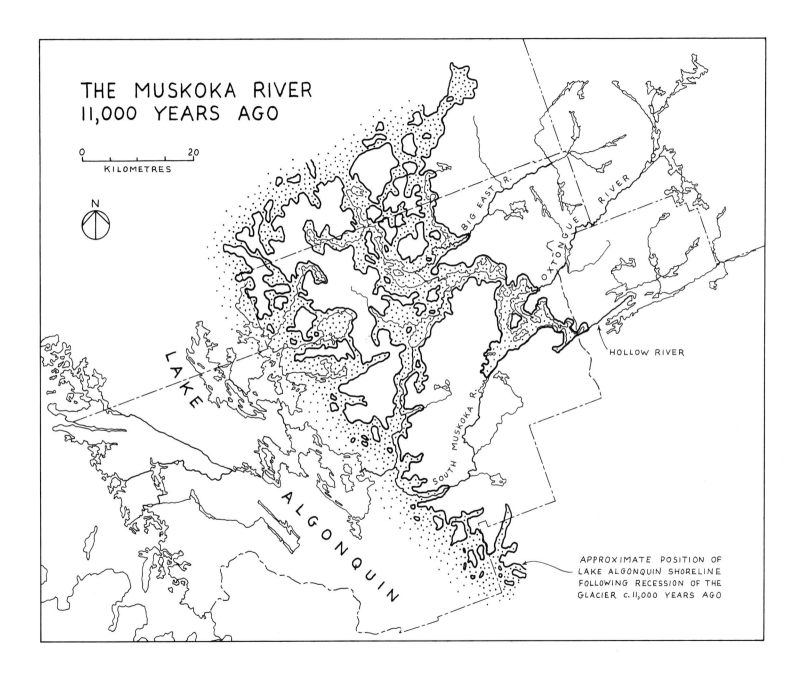

THE MUSKOKA RIVER
11,000 YEARS AGO

0   20
KILOMETRES

N

BIG EAST R.

OXTONGUE RIVER

HOLLOW RIVER

LAKE

SOUTH MUSKOKA R.

ALGONQUIN

APPROXIMATE POSITION OF
LAKE ALGONQUIN SHORELINE
FOLLOWING RECESSION OF THE
GLACIER c. 11,000 YEARS AGO

koka River valley from the South Falls area; the North Muskoka valley formed part of a long, winding strait and series of large bays extending up through the Huntsville Lakes and the Buck and Little East River valleys. This passage separated the mainland to the east from a huge offshore island that stretched from just north of Bracebridge to beyond the northern boundary of Muskoka District. Lake of Bays was connected to Lake Algonquin by a strait through a narrow gap in the hills east of Peninsula Lake. Due to the depression of the land, that gap was slightly lower than the Baysville outlet of Lake of Bays when the receding glacier exposed it (now it's about eight metres higher).

At the time the ice was still receding from the North and South Muskoka River valleys, raging meltwater spillways surged down them into the main body of Lake Algonquin. As a result, extensive outwash and deltaic deposits of gravel, sand and silt accumulated along the valleys and around their mouths in the Bracebridge and Muskoka Airport areas.

As the ice continued its northward retreat the Hollow, Oxtongue and Big East rivers took their turns as major spillways pouring down off the Algonquin Highland into Lake Algonquin and Lake of Bays. Large deltas formed at their mouths near Dorset, Dwight and Huntsville, and thick deposits of sand and gravel were laid down along the Big East and Oxtongue valleys.

Thick clay deposits that built up on what was once the bottom of Lake Algonquin (notably in the Bracebridge, Huntsville and Three Mile Lake areas) point to a fairly long period of inundation during and after the ice recession across Muskoka — at least 800 years. These clays are composed of the finest particles carried down by glacial meltwaters and subsequent normal run-off.

At the time the ice uncovered the Muskoka watershed, Lake Algonquin drained eastward down the Trent River valley through an outlet at Fenelon Falls (and also southward through outlets at Sarnia and Chicago). As the ice front withdrew further north it uncovered a succession of lower outlets around the north side of the Algonquin Dome into the Ottawa River. The lowest of these, the North Bay outlet, followed a route down the Mattawa River. Through it Lake Algonquin drained down quite rapidly, in just a few centuries, to a level nearly 120 metres (395 feet) below the current elevations of Georgian Bay, Lake Huron and Lake Michigan. At that stage, about 10,400 years ago, the shore of Georgian Bay was several kilometres west of the present mouths of the Muskoka River and thus the Muskoka was longer than it is today. The river had, of course, extended itself westward as Lake Algonquin dropped and receded.

The low water stage didn't last long. As the land under the North Bay outlet rebounded, faster than the land to the south, water levels in the Georgian Bay, Huron and Michigan basins rose. By about 5,500 years ago they had risen more or less back to the original level of Lake Algonquin and discharge began again through the Sarnia and Chicago outlets. The North Bay outlet subsequently dried up as it continued to rise.

In the meantime the Muskoka River watershed had been rising too, so the new high water levels flooded only the lower reaches of the Moon and Musquash River valleys and lands close to Georgian Bay. This high water period, known as the Nipissing stage, persisted until about 3,500 years ago. Subsequent erosion of the Sarnia outlet (the present outlet of Lake Huron) allowed water levels to fall more or less to their current elevation.

The centuries immediately after the retreat of the ice and the subsequent recession of the Lake Algonquin waters was the time during which the Muskoka River system evolved most rapidly towards its present form. The thick glacial meltwater deposits that had accumulated in the bedrock valleys fell easy prey to erosion as normal creeks and rivers began to develop. The North and South Muskoka, the Big East, the Oxtongue and dozens of smaller streams cut down into the sands, gravels and clays, essentially carving new valleys within valleys. They carried huge quantities of eroded materials downstream and redeposited them as deltas where they entered such lakes as Muskoka, Vernon and Lake of Bays.

When the streams had dug down far enough (often in excess of 30 metres, or 100 feet) they uncovered the rock sills separating the basins the glaciers had excavated in the bedrock underneath. Waterfalls thundered to life over these. In between, the streams continued to erode their channels and evolve their meandering courses. Evidence that rivers once flowed at much higher levels and carried greater quantities of water than they do now exists in many parts of the Muskoka watershed in the form of old river banks and terraces well beyond or above the present channels.

Many parts of the Muskoka River watershed received only scant deposits of loose glacially-derived materials; not surprisingly, streams in these areas attained their modern characteristics very soon after their valleys were exposed. The Moon and Musquash rivers are prime examples of that. Of course, the hundreds of lakes in the watershed also testify to the often meagre surficial deposits left as a result of glaciation. The majority of the lakes exist because water, not glacial drift, filled the basins carved into the bedrock by the ice. Chains of lakes rather than normal stream channels comprise the drainage through numerous sections of the Muskoka River system.

Many of the lakes in the Muskoka watershed — including big ones like the Muskoka Lakes, the Huntsville Lakes, Lake of Bays, and Skeleton, Three Mile and Mary lakes — were initially drowned by Lake Algonquin. They were simply left behind when Lake Algonquin receded, their volumes retained in bedrock basins.

Throughout the Muskoka watershed the courses of creeks and rivers and the size and shape of lakes are largely determined by the bedrock topography, the pattern of ridges and valleys, hills and basins. This isn't always evident on the ground because channels and shorelines themselves are frequently formed in sand, gravel or clay. However, you need only examine a topographic map or aerial photograph to see the overwhelming extent to which the waterways follow the grooves between the ridges or the lines of the numerous ancient faults that cut across the landscape.

Still in its infancy, the Muskoka River has not yet made much headway towards imposing its own will on the rock that controls its course. It blindly follows whatever valleys and hollows the bedrock topography provides. This creates the interesting anomaly of diverging waterways in the western part of the watershed, where the Musquash River flows out of the Moon and the Go Home out of the Musquash (each, incidentally, following old fault lines). The glaciers just happened to erode the channels around the points of divergence close enough to the same depth that both carry water. In the natural course of river evolution, one channel would erode down faster than the other and take all of the water. In the case of the Moon, Musquash and Go Home, dams have halted that process for the time being.

The bedrock under the watershed controls not just the direction but also the descent of the Muskoka River. The initial period of rapid erosion into loose glacial meltwater deposits came to an abrupt end when streams encountered that very hard billion-year-old gneiss. When such rock became exposed in stream channels at waterfalls or at the outlets of lakes, it severely curtailed the ability of the streams to continue their natural work of erosion. Held up by hard rock sills, many stretches of deep, stable channel evolved where the current normally flows so gently that these reaches can almost be regarded as long, narrow lakes.

Of course, we do have streams like the lower Big East River with valleys so clogged with sand and silt that they're still rapidly evolving, digging down, constantly altering their wildly meandering courses, and actively constructing deltas where they enter lakes. But on the whole, the Muskoka River system is evolving very slowly now.

Rivers never stop evolving. Quickly or slowly, from the moment of their birth they wear constantly at the rock and soil, changing the landscape and in the process developing new characteristics of their own. Water descending from higher to lower elevations represents a conversion of energy to work. The current tears away and carries the looser materials, the eroded particles gradually abrade the rock, waterfalls pound relentlessly. Over millions of years rivers move entire mountains down into the lakes and seas.

Given enough time the Muskoka River will eliminate the irregularities in its channels where waterfalls now tumble, and fill in the basins that contain the big lakes. Some day it may resemble its ancestors, the rivers that drained this part of the country before the Ice Age. But who knows? Long before that, some dramatic event — another continental glacier, perhaps — could well intervene and set the river on an entirely new course.

BIG BEND, Big East River. This dramatic 23-metre-high (75-foot) erosion bank exposes layers of deltaic sands and silts deposited some 11,000 years ago by a raging glacial meltwater spillway where it entered Lake Algonquin. The Big East has been carving down into these deposits ever since.

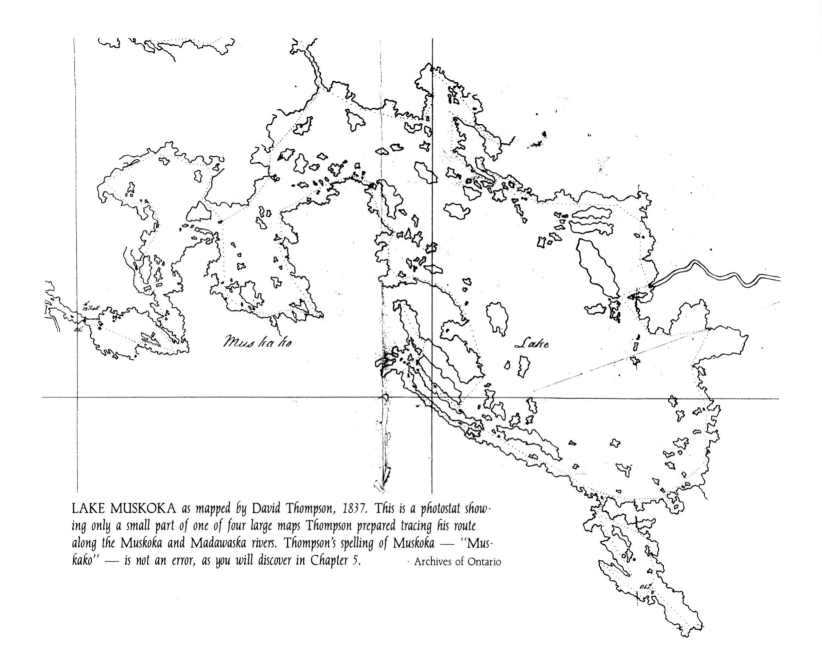

Mus ka ko

Lake

LAKE MUSKOKA as mapped by David Thompson, 1837. This is a photostat showing only a small part of one of four large maps Thompson prepared tracing his route
along the Muskoka and Madawaska rivers. Thompson's spelling of Muskoka — "Muskako" — is not an error, as you will discover in Chapter 5.   · Archives of Ontario

CHAPTER 4

In the Wake of the Canoe: Early Explorers on the Muskoka River

Just over a century and a quarter ago, in 1859, settlement officially began in the Muskoka River watershed. Only 33 years before that, in 1826, the first explorers ventured onto the river — the first, that is, to leave a written record.

Prior to 1826, the Muskoka and many of the other rivers draining the huge tract of wilderness climbing over the Algonquin Dome were known only to Indian hunters and trappers and a handful of white fur traders who paddled these waters in the course of their activities; none of these early travellers apparently left any lasting record of their journeys. The Algonquin Dome was a rough, lake-strewn island that remained officially unexplored despite a flurry of European activity all around it dating back to the early 1600s.

In 1610, just two years after Samuel de Champlain founded Quebec, a young Frenchman named Etienne Brûlé accompanied some Huron Indians to their homeland in Huronia, the area between Georgian Bay and Lake Simcoe just south of Muskoka District. From Quebec they canoed up the St. Lawrence and Ottawa rivers, crossed to Georgian Bay along the Mattawa River, Lake Nipissing and the French River, then paddled down the east shore of Georgian Bay to their destination. Not long afterwards, in 1615, Samuel de Champlain himself nearly circled the Algonquin Dome. He travelled to Huronia by the same route Brûlé had taken, then, by way of Lake Simcoe and the Trent River system, accompanied the

Hurons on an incursion into hostile Iroquois country south of Lake Ontario.

Apparently no Indians lived permanently in the Muskoka River watershed just north of Huronia at that time. This area, and land extending far to the north beyond Lake Nipissing, was part of the territory of the Algonquin Indians, a nomadic people who hunted, fished, and traded furs to the Hurons. The Hurons led a more settled existence. They cultivated a few crops and traded furs, obtained from the Algonquins, with the French at Quebec. They first began journeying to Quebec in 1609, using the long northern route via the French, Mattawa and Ottawa rivers. They did not use, perhaps did not know of, the river connections to the east provided by the Muskoka and other streams of the Algonquin Dome.

Up until 1649 French Jesuit missionaries were active in Huronia, where they maintained permanent missions. The Jesuits also ventured up the Georgian Bay coast and into Lake Nipissing to minister to the Algonquins; they apparently carried out little, if any, work in the interior of the Algonquin Dome.

In 1649 the Iroquois from the south massacred the Huron nation and the Jesuits working there in a bid to take over the fur-rich hinterland north of Lake Ontario. The Iroquois traded with the English and Dutch on what is now the

United States eastern seaboard. For a time after their conquest of the Hurons, they hunted and trapped in the Muskoka area. However, they couldn't maintain an invincible hold on the land north of Lake Ontario, and from 1669 onwards French explorers and fur traders traversed the country immediately south of Muskoka.

Notable among these explorers was René Robert Cavalier, sieur de La Salle. Three or four times he paddled along the Severn River between Lake Simcoe and Georgian Bay (on one of these occasions, in 1682, he embarked on a journey that would take him all the way to the mouth of the Mississippi River). The French recognized the strategic importance of the Severn as part of a shortcut from Lake Ontario to Georgian Bay. They reached Lake Simcoe and the Severn primarily by way of a portage starting near the present site of Toronto.

Along the east and north sides of the Algonquin Dome, the Ottawa-Mattawa-French River route continued to serve French explorers and fur traders. Later this would become part of the famous fur-trade route between Montreal and western Canada. Still, no official forays were made into the interior of the Dome, certainly not into the Muskoka River watershed. It's possible that some *coureurs de bois*, independent French fur traders, canoed on the Muskoka and other Dome rivers, but as they were engaged in illegal trade, they didn't readily publicize their activities.

It was well known during the French period that extensive waterways existed in the wilds of the Algonquin Dome. Maps from the 1600s show lakes and rivers in the region. One published in 1657 shows a lake somewhat like Lake Muskoka in outline, drained by a forking pair of rivers bearing a certain resemblance to the Moon and Musquash. Information for such maps came from Indians, missionaries, perhaps some of the *coureurs de bois*, and when hard facts were lacking, from the imagination of the cartographer.

Even after the British gained control of Canada from the French in 1763, no official interest was shown in the Algonquin Dome for quite some time. However, both French and British fur traders operating up through Lake Simcoe, and later from Penetanguishene on Georgian Bay as well, paddled into the Muskoka River system, where they set up temporary summer camps to obtain furs from the Ojibwa Indians, who had migrated from further to the northwest. The Ojibwa only hunted and trapped in Muskoka; they lived in the Lake Simcoe area.

THE CANAL ROUTE EXPLORATIONS

In the end, it was trouble with the Americans that set in motion the train of events that would lead to the first important exploratory expeditions on the Muskoka River.

After the American Revolution (1775-1783), the resulting hostility between the British in Canada and the Americans caused the British military to begin looking for a better water route from the St. Lawrence - Lake Ontario area to Georgian Bay and the upper Great Lakes. The southern route up through Lake Erie was too close to the Americans (and in any case impeded by Niagara Falls) and the fur-trade route along the Ottawa, Mattawa and French rivers was interrupted by numerous waterfalls and rapids. Interest therefore focused on a central route through Lake Simcoe and the Severn River. At least two British expeditions examined that region in subsequent years, although the numerous waterfalls on the Severn did raise some doubts about that stream's suitability as a water route.

The War of 1812 between Canada and the United States re-emphasized the need for a water route not vulnerable to American attack. One possibility was a canal using the Trent and Severn River systems between Lake Ontario and Georgian Bay. Another was a canal following as yet unexplored waterways along the southern fringe of the Algonquin Dome between the Ottawa River and Georgian Bay. In the course of investigating the latter idea, British military expeditions commanded by Royal Engineers would make the first documented journeys along several rivers, including the Muskoka.

It was thought that the Severn River could serve as the western outlet of the proposed canal, so in 1819 Lieutenant Joseph Portlock examined that stream and reported on ways to overcome its waterfalls and rapids by means of dams and canals. Also in 1819, Lieutenant James Catty began the more difficult task of finding a route eastward from Lake Simcoe and the Severn to the Ottawa River. Using the Talbot, Gull, Drag, York and Madawaska rivers he canoed and portaged all the way from Lake Simcoe to the Ottawa. He found the country difficult, the rivers impeded by many falls and rapids; in his opinion the route was unsuited for canalization.

Undaunted by Catty's report, the British military dispatched more expeditions led by Royal Engineers to explore these waterways a few years later. In 1826 Lieutenants William Marlow and William Smith canoed up part of the previously unexplored Black River (which flows into the Severn at Washago), then returned to Lake Simcoe via the Gull and Talbot rivers. They found the Black too broken by falls to be of any use as part of a canal scheme. The Talbot suffered a number of impediments to navigation as well, but it quickly became regarded as a possible link between Lake Simcoe and the Trent River system. Indeed, it later became part of the Trent-Severn waterway connecting Lake Ontario with Georgian Bay.

Lieutenant Henry Briscoe, the man originally instructed to explore the Black and Talbot rivers in 1826, failed to do so. Frustrated in his attempts to secure an Indian guide for those routes, he finally hired one who could take him on a more northerly route along a large river that eventually gave access to the eastward-flowing Madawaska. That large river was the Muskoka, and Lieutenant Henry Briscoe, quite by accident, became the first man to travel on it and leave a written record of the expedition.

Although very brief and containing no description of the surrounding country, Briscoe's account of his Muskoka River trip is detailed enough that we can easily trace his route. The party reached the Muskoka along a well-known Indian canoe route that led up Morrison Creek from the Severn River to Muldrew Lake, thence across a three-kilometre (2 mile) portage that came out on Lake Muskoka near the present site of the Gravenhurst wharf. Arriving on Lake Muskoka on September 7 or 8, 1826, Briscoe then took about two weeks to ascend the river to the height of land on the Algonquin Highland, using the South Muskoka and Oxtongue rivers. From there he portaged from Big Porcupine Lake over into the headwaters of the Madawaska, which he descended for a way before portaging to the Petawawa to complete his descent to the Ottawa.

Briscoe either didn't know of any name given to the Muskoka River, or didn't report it. The crude map of the waterways he followed names only two features on the Muskoka: Sault du Sauvage (South Falls) and Lake Baptiste (Lake of Bays). Briscoe's report and the map are both reprinted in the book *Muskoka and Haliburton*, edited by Florence B. Murray.

This excellent reference work contains excerpts from the diaries and reports of many early Muskoka River explorers, as well as documents relating to virtually all other aspects of Muskoka history from 1615 to 1875.

Briscoe's "discovery" of the Muskoka River apparently didn't excite the British military authorities, possibly because the river didn't fall into Lake Simcoe or the Severn. In 1827 Briscoe was ordered to repeat his ascent of the Muskoka, which he did, but the main purpose of the expedition was to re-examine part of Catty's 1819 route. Also in 1827 Lieutenant John Walpole followed Catty's route again in its entirety, along the Talbot, Gull, Drag, York and Madawaska rivers. Walpole was equally negative about the suitability of this route for a canal. Even the large Madawaska River was so broken by rapids that it was virtually useless for transportation.

The discouraging reports of the difficult country and precipitous descents along the Algonquin Dome rivers no doubt helps explain why the British military sent out no more expeditions after 1827 to find a route for a canal across this highland. The idea of such a canal was far from dead, however, and would soon lead to another important exploratory expedition on the Muskoka River. This one was a private venture instigated and undertaken by the Shirreff family.

In the 1820s entrepreneur Charles Shirreff of Fitzroy Harbour (on the Ottawa River) learned from fur traders of a water route, clearly following the Petawawa and Muskoka rivers, that seemed suitable for a canal across the Algonquin Dome. Aside from the military advantages, Shirreff suggested that such a canal would open up a vast tract of land for settlement and lumbering. As well, by providing a shorter route from the upper Great Lakes to the east, it would regain for the St. Lawrence the trade from the rapidly expanding American midwest, trade being lost through the new Erie Canal running from Lake Erie to the Hudson River system, which drains south to New York City.

Shirreff proposed that a private company build the canal and be granted Crown lands to sell along the route to help finance it. One of his sons, Robert, was interested in setting up a land company to settle the Algonquin Dome territory. But before anything definite could be done, it was necessary to explore the proposed canal route and examine the country along it. This task fell to another of Shirreff's sons, Alexander, who had been working on the Rideau Canal for Lieutenant-Colonel John By. (Colonel By, incidentally, thought very highly of Shirreff's water route and even suggested that a ship canal could be built along it for £800,000 — that without ever having seen the country!)

Alexander Shirreff undertook the exploratory expedition in the late summer and early fall of 1829. He gives us the first detailed description of the Muskoka River and the land it flows through (the relevant parts of his account are reprinted in *Muskoka and Haliburton*). Unfortunately, he made the mistake of thinking that the hardwood forests covering the hills indicated rich soil, an error that would be perpetuated for decades.

Unlike Briscoe, Shirreff entered the Muskoka River watershed from the east, through Tom Thomson Lake, after coming up the Petawawa. He followed the Oxtongue, South Muskoka and Musquash rivers all the way down to Georgian Bay. He then came up the Severn, crossed back to Lake Muskoka via Morrison Creek and the Muldrew portage, and returned to the Algonquin Highland along the South Muskoka and Oxtongue. From Smoke Lake he portaged over into the headwaters of the Madawaska and used that stream rather than the Petawawa to descend eastward to the Ottawa River.

Shirreff was impressed by the land along the Muskoka, by the quality of the water and by the potential for inland navigation provided by the lakes. Evidently, though, he didn't find the route suitable for a canal, for that idea didn't appear in subsequent land company settlement proposals. Even the idea of settling the Algonquin Dome was soon abandoned, when the government decided not to allow such development at that time.

Alexander Shirreff made several notable contributions to Muskoka River history. Aside from his excellent description, he no doubt supplied much of the information for a map published in 1834 which gives the first recognizable renderings of the Muskoka River system. He was also the first to record the use of the name Muskoka for the river.

One of the most significant Muskoka River explorations — and the last of the canal route expeditions — took place in 1837. The idea that a canal route might be found between Georgian Bay and the Ottawa River just wouldn't die. Perhaps seeking to lay the matter to rest once and for all, in 1837 the government of Upper Canada (Ontario) appointed a commission to study the problem. The commission subsequently hired three surveyors to explore the numerous potential water routes between Georgian Bay and the Ottawa River. The man they chose to investigate the Muskoka River, along with the Madawaska, was none other than David Thompson.

Today we recognize David Thompson as one of the foremost explorers, surveyors and cartographers in Canadian history. From the 1790s to 1812, in the course of his work as a fur trader (mostly with the North West Company, in which he became a partner), he surveyed and mapped several million square kilometres of the Canadian west. Such was the extent and accuracy of his work that his maps formed the basis for all maps of that vast region for a century afterwards. Among his other achievements, Thompson established the first fur-trading post on the Columbia River and became the first white man to travel that mighty stream from its source to its mouth. The Thompson River in British Columbia is named for him.

As so often happens with great achievers, Thompson never received the recognition he deserved during his lifetime, and he died in poverty. The wealth of information and fine maps that resulted from his work on the Muskoka River, for instance, was virtually forgotten for decades.

Thompson was 67 years old when he undertook the Muskoka River survey. Nonetheless, he tackled the job with the same dedication, thoroughness and accuracy that characterized his better-known exploits in the West. He produced the first systematic and accurate survey of the river, recorded a wealth of data on courses, distances and elevations, and drew two excellent maps showing the lakes and streams he explored.

Thompson spent nearly two months on the Muskoka, in August and September of 1837. From Georgian Bay he worked his way up the Musquash, the South Muskoka and the Oxtongue before portaging from Big Porcupine Lake into the Madawaska River system. On the way he traversed the shores of all three Muskoka Lakes, Lake of Bays and some of the Oxtongue headwater lakes. Excerpts from his diary are included in *Muskoka and Haliburton*.

Apparently, before he even started, Thompson realized that a canal route could never be established across the lofty

Algonquin Dome. His survey of the Muskoka merely confirmed that the huge descent and scores of waterfalls that would have to be overcome would make such a scheme unfeasible. It's worth noting that the lowest point on the height of land between the Muskoka and the eastward-flowing rivers of the Algonquin Dome is some 252 metres (827 feet) above Georgian Bay. Compare that with little more than 30 metres (100 feet) along the French-Mattawa River route further north, where canal schemes have been proposed at various times, although never acted upon. No further interest was shown for a canal route along the Muskoka.

Although Thompson didn't think much of the Muskoka River's canal potential, the land along the river impressed him more favourably. In a letter to the government in 1840 he noted that his expedition had brought to light a valuable tract of land for settlement. Like Alexander Shirreff, he mistook the hardwood forests of the watershed as an indication of rich soil (as indeed they were to the south of the Shield). His observation that the abundance of waterfalls would serve well as mill sites, however, was right on the mark. Thompson advocated an immediate detailed survey of the land along the Muskoka and the other rivers flowing into the east side of Georgian Bay, with settlement to proceed forthwith. Little heed was paid to that suggestion, but that did not mean the government had no interest in the resources and settlement potential of watersheds on the Algonquin Dome. It did, and the interest grew as the years passed.

EXPLORATIONS FOR RESOURCES AND DEVELOPMENT

Although the examination of the Muskoka River as a possible canal route was a major reason for Alexander Shirreff's 1829 expedition, Shirreff had a second important objective: to determine the suitability of the surrounding land for settlement and development. As such his trip heralded the beginning of more widespread interest in the wilderness north of the districts bordering Lake Ontario, which were becoming increasingly populated. The rivers and lakes of the Muskoka River system provided convenient highways for men sent out to examine the resources of the region, and later for surveyors, when the government decided to open townships in the watershed for settlement.

Five years after Shirreff's trip, the government of Upper Canada decided to initiate a large-scale exploratory survey of the rivers and lands on the Georgian Bay side of the Algonquin Dome, including the Muskoka River and its watershed. The objective was to run a survey line north through the area from just east of Lake Couchiching, explore the lands and waterways, and report on the resources and potential of the region. The work was carried out in the summer and fall of 1835, two years before David Thompson's expedition. It produced much valuable new information about the region, but little in the way of maps of the Muskoka River.

The leader of the expedition, Lieutenant John Carthew (Royal Navy), and party geologist Lieutenant Frederick Baddeley (Royal Engineers) independently explored several lakes and rivers in the western part of the Muskoka watershed: the lower two thirds of the South Muskoka, Lake Muskoka, and the Musquash River. Baddeley went up the North Muskoka as far as Bracebridge Falls, the first recorded visit to that site. Carthew broke new ground, officially at least, by ascending the Indian River to Lake Rosseau, then continuing up the Dee River into Three Mile Lake. Carthew also visited Skeleton Lake, which the party surveyors had encountered in the path of their survey line. Carthew provides the first known descriptions of Rosseau, Skeleton and Three Mile lakes.

Frederick Baddeley was impressed by the forests and by the water-power potential of the waterfalls. However, he considered Alexander Shirreff's conclusion that the fine hardwood forests indicated rich soil to be misleading; he reported the soil generally sandy and very thin.

Except for David Thompson's 1837 canal exploration, no further official exploration of the Muskoka watershed occurred until the late 1840s (fur traders, however, continued to operate in the region). By then the government of Canada (Upper and Lower Canada, Ontario and Quebec, had been amalgamated in 1841) had initiated further surveys along the southern fringe of the Algonquin Dome. Surveyor Robert Bell ran an east-west line in 1847-48 that terminated at the Muskoka River near the present site of Bracebridge. While in the area in February 1848, Bell journeyed up the North Muskoka (on foot) past High Falls, the first recorded trip that far up. He also visited South Falls on the South Muskoka. It impressed him so much — he called it the Great Falls — that he recommended a townsite be established there.

Bell, like Baddeley and Thompson before him, commented on the water-power potential of the Muskoka River. In that era water power was still an important consideration with regard to the establishment of industry. Surveyor James Bridgland also noted the water powers on an 1852 survey in southwestern Muskoka; so too did the surveyors who would soon begin surveying the townships of Muskoka for settlement. Bridgland, however, considered the land along the Muskoka River almost entirely unfit for settlement and recommended against it. The government ignored that recommendation.

The last major exploration of the Muskoka River took place in 1853. That year the Geological Survey of Canada (established in 1841) sent Alexander Murray out to study the geology of the Canadian Shield between Georgian Bay and the Ottawa River. Murray decided that the river systems offered the easiest means of traversing the territory. He started off by paddling up the Musquash River and around Lake Muskoka. Continuing eastward, he chose to ascend the North Muskoka rather than take the usual route up the South Muskoka, and as a result he made the first recorded visits to Mary, Fairy and Peninsula lakes. He didn't follow the North Muskoka west as far as Lake Vernon; instead, he turned east into Peninsula Lake, from which he portaged over into Lake of Bays. After traversing the shores of that big lake, he ascended the Oxtongue River, passing through Tea, Canoe, Joe and Burnt Island lakes before crossing the height of land into the Petawawa River system.

Out of Murray's expedition came not only the first descriptions of three of the big lakes on the North Muskoka, but also some remarkably accurate measurements of the heights of several waterfalls along the route he took. In addition, Murray named seven lakes in the watershed, names still in use today (more about that in Chapter 5). His report (reprinted in *Muskoka and Haliburton*) provides an informative and interesting description of the lands and waterways he saw. Murray was one of the last men to see the entire river in its virgin wilderness state; not long afterwards the lumber companies began their assault on the watershed.

As late as the 1850s several significant parts of the Muskoka watershed still hadn't been officially explored, notably the Big East, Buck and Hollow rivers. These streams, however, had undoubtedly been known and visited by fur traders for many years. The explorers hadn't used them because they didn't provide convenient canoe routes to and from the east. Over the next three decades a great influx of lumbermen, settlers, surveyors and trappers to the Muskoka watershed would fill in the last remaining blank spaces on the maps of the waterways and lakes.

Surveyor John Dennis "discovered" Lake Vernon and the Big East River in 1860. By then the government had begun pushing a colonization road, the Muskoka Road, north from Washago into the Muskoka wilderness, and had opened some land east and south of Lake Muskoka for settlement. In 1858 the Muskoka Road survey progressed as far north as South Falls; in 1860 Dennis was to continue the road survey north through what is now Huntsville.

Before he started the survey, Dennis felt it necessary to do a canoe traverse of the North Muskoka River and the Muskoka Lakes to get an accurate idea of their position and extent. He also went down the Musquash River to examine the harbour at its mouth. Had he known of the existence of David Thompson's precise 1837 maps, Dennis could have saved himself much of this exploratory work. In the process of these explorations Dennis became the first known (though not the first) white man to see Lake Vernon and the lower Big East River. He also "rediscovered" Lake Joseph. Although Thompson had mapped it in 1837, this large lake remained virtually unknown in official circles until 1860.

Two exploratory trips on the Muskoka River after 1860 deserve mention, not so much for new discoveries made, but for their consequences. In the fall of 1865 a young man named Alexander Peter Cockburn from Kirkfield, Ontario, made an extensive canoe trip that began at Dorset, took him across Lake of Bays, Peninsula and Fairy lakes, then up through Lake Vernon and the Buck River system to the Magnetawan River to the north. That same fall he also toured the Muskoka Lakes. As a result of these explorations Cockburn was sufficiently impressed by Muskoka's potential that he decided to put a steamboat on the Muskoka Lakes. That decision would have far-reaching benefits for Muskoka District.

Equally far-reaching benefits eventually accrued from the activities of another man, provincial land surveyor James Dickson. Through the 1880s Dickson conducted extensive surveys and explorations of the waterways and land in the headwaters of the Muskoka River, as well as in the headwaters of other rivers originating on the Algonquin Highland. These started out as a continuation of Ontario government plans to open up more land on the Algonquin Dome for settlement, but soon they took on a very different purpose: examination of the area preliminary to setting it aside as a park.

The idea of a large park on the Algonquin Highland had been put forward in 1885 by an employee in the Crown Lands Department, Alexander Kirkwood. He was concerned about the consequences of the destruction of forests by settlers and lumbermen, and persuaded the government to consider his proposal. Before any sort of park could be established, however, it was necessary to gain an accurate idea of the resources of the region in question, particularly to determine that it was indeed unsuited for settlement. James Dickson was chosen for that job; by good fortune he also strongly favoured a park on the Algonquin Highland.

Largely as a result of the work of Dickson and Kirkwood, the Ontario government established Algonquin Park in 1893. One of its most important purposes was protection of the headwaters of the Muskoka and the other rivers draining off the Algonquin Highland.

In a book he wrote (*Camping in the Muskoka Region*) James Dickson gives an interesting account of a canoe trip up the Oxtongue River and through the headwater lakes. It provides one of the last glimpses of the waterways and forests of the area before the lumbermen moved in a few years later and wrought their great changes on the last remaining virgin wilderness in the Muskoka River watershed.

We can still explore the Muskoka River today and discover new things — new at least in our own experience — but in light of over 130 years of development on the river, and with the knowledge of the birth and evolution of the river not available to early explorers, we can now indulge in the highly satisfying exploration of the Muskoka River's past.

UPPER DISTRESS CHUTE, Big East River. Not nearly as well known as more accessible parts of Muskoka, the upper Big East River offers some of the wildest and finest scenery in the Muskoka watershed.

CHAPTER 5

Muskoka or Muskako? Naming the Lakes, Streams and Waterfalls

If you examine a reasonably detailed map you cannot help but be impressed by the diversity of names given to the lakes, creeks, rivers, waterfalls and other features of the Muskoka River system. No doubt you will begin to wonder how some of them came about. There's a story behind every name, if not in the name itself then in the people or circumstances surrounding it.

Most of the names in use today on the Muskoka River date back to the latter 19th century. That was the period of the largest initial influx of surveyors, settlers, trappers, lumbermen and vacationers to an area that up until then had been sparsely inhabited wilderness. In the absence of existing official names, it was only natural that they would themselves name the landscape features that figured so prominently in their lives. The names of some of the major lakes and streams, however, can be traced back to the earlier fur-trading and exploration days. And at the other end of the time scale, a slow evolution of names continues even to this day.

Of course, long before Europeans arrived in the Muskoka River watershed, the Indians who hunted and trapped in the area had already named many lakes and streams. Those often colourful and perceptive Indian names, unfortunately, were not usually retained and in many cases no record of them remains.

The names of many elements of the river system, especially the lakes, reflect components of the natural environment: the birds, the mammals, the fish, and the trees and plants of the forests and waters of the region. A great many others were suggested by the physical nature or character of the lake, stream or waterfall they identify: High Falls, Ragged Falls, Shadow River, Clear Lake, Burnt Island Lake, Peninsula Lake . . . . Trappers and lumbermen working in areas that had not been settled were perhaps the most prolific in naming features after natural attributes.

In the settled central part of the watershed many names belong to the pioneers who homesteaded on the shores of lakes and streams or built mills at waterfalls: smaller lakes and streams such as Young, Dickie and Walker lakes, Jessop's and Ballantine's creeks; and important waterfalls like Wilson's Falls, Hanna Chute, Trethewey Falls, Matthias Falls and Marsh's Falls. Sprinkled about the watershed we find features that immortalize fur traders, lumbermen, Indians and others associated with the history of the river and the district. Notable examples include Sandy Gray's Chute on the Musquash River, named for a log driver who drowned when the log-jam he was trying to free suddenly gave way; Lake Rosseau, named for an early fur trader; and Bigwin Island in Lake of Bays, which was once part of the hunting territory of Chief John Bigwin and his people. A lake in the Oxtongue headwaters was renamed Tom Thomson Lake in honour of the noted Canadian artist who drowned in nearby Canoe Lake in 1917.

It was not uncommon to name things in honour of loved ones or associates — Mary Lake and Lake Joseph stand out in that regard. Sometimes geographic features back in the "old country" inspired a name — the Dee River, for instance. Dozens of names merely come from the community or township in which the feature is located. Waterfalls at Bracebridge, Bala and Port Sydney, and lakes in Finlayson, McCraney and Medora townships all fall into this category, and there are other examples.

Many interesting names commemorate an event or circumstance of the past. For instance, we have Whisky Rapids on the Oxtongue River, named, so the story goes, when two slightly inebriated log drivers upset their canoe in them and lost a keg of whisky; the Long Slide chute on the Hollow River, once by-passed by a huge log slide; and the Distress Dam and Chutes on the Big East River, the precise origins unclear but undoubtedly intriguing (it dates back to the log-driving era). Canoe Lake, Skeleton Lake, Go Home Lake and Trading Bay are all names that reflect events of the past too (more about these shortly).

The oldest name associated with the Muskoka River that is still in use today is, appropriately, Muskoka. Fur traders apparently coined the name by the 1820s. Alexander Shirreff, who explored the Muskoka River in 1829, first recorded it. He wrote, "This river, by the traders, is called the Muskoka, after the Mississauga chief, who hunts in some part of its neighbourhood. The Indians have some other name for it, which I could not learn . . ."

The Indian chief Shirreff refers to is William Yellowhead,

Chief Mesqua Ukie. He headed a band of Chippewa (Ojibwa) Indians who at the time lived around the present site of Orillia but hunted in the area from Lake Muskoka to Lake of Bays.

While it is generally accepted that Chief Mesqua Ukie inspired the name Muskoka, other explanations of its origin exist. For instance, David Thompson referred to the stream on his 1837 expedition as the "Muskako," short for *Muska ko skow see pie*, an Indian name meaning Swamp Ground River. The Muskoka River isn't generally swampy, but perhaps the name derives from the extensive marshy and swampy areas around its mouth at Lake Muskoka.

Early explorers used the name Muskoka for the entire length of the river, from its headwaters on the Algonquin Highland right down to Georgian Bay, following the main canoe route along the Oxtongue, South Muskoka and Musquash rivers. Not until years later did the various sections get their own names.

West of Lake Muskoka, the Musquash River became known as such in the early 1870s. Musquash, a word of Algonquin origins, is another name for the muskrat. These mammals apparently lived in some abundance in the river's environs. The other branch of the Muskoka River below Lake Muskoka, the Moon River, may have started out as the Moose. In 1829 Alexander Shirreff's father, Charles, referred to a Moose River which was almost certainly part of the Muskoka River system, and so-named by fur traders. The name Moon appears six years later in government instructions to the Carthew-Baddeley exploration party. We can hypothesize that the similarity of sound led to an accidental change from Moose to Moon. There is still a Moose Point on Georgian Bay not far from the mouth of the Moon River.

An Indian village at the present site of Port Carling up until the mid-1860s logically explains why early settlers or surveyors gave the name Indian to the important waterway linking Lake Rosseau with Lake Muskoka. Some surveyors at first called it the Rosseau River, a name soon applied exclusively instead to a smaller tributary to Lake Rosseau.

It's quite obvious why the North and South branches of the Muskoka became so known. Although the North Branch had always been called that, not until after settlement began did the South Branch become generally recognized as just a major tributary and not a continuation of the mainstream Muskoka.

The principal headwater of the South Muskoka, the Oxtongue River, was still frequently referred to as the Muskoka as late as the early 1900s. The name Oxtongue, taken from the lake through which the river passes, began creeping into use by 1890. The other major headwater of the South Muskoka, the Hollow River, gets its name from the lake out of which it flows: Hollow Lake (later Kawagama Lake).

The Big East River, main headwater of the North Muskoka, started out simply as the East River, a name used by surveyors and settlers in the 1860s probably because of the river's source in the east. Surveyor John Dennis made the first recorded visit to the lower Big East in 1860; one of his assistants, Vernon B. Wadsworth, later wrote that Dennis had discovered the ''East Sand River,'' an obvious reference to the sandy nature of the stream. Although East River is still the official name, everybody in the district knows this flood-prone river today as the Big East. John Dennis, incidentally, named Lake Vernon after Wadsworth.

The man who first recorded the use of the name Muskoka in 1829, Alexander Shirreff, was at the same time the first to use that name for the largest lake in the watershed, Lake

Muskoka. In 1835 Frederick Baddeley noted that while Shirreff had called it Muskoka, his party was informed (presumably by Indians) that it was called *Chimie* or *Kitshisagan*. The latter meant Big Mouth of the River — appropriate, since the lake receives the Muskoka River from the east. In 1837 David Thompson referred to the lake as *Mus ka ko skow, oo, Lak a hagan* (Swamp Ground, Its Lake).

To the north, Lake Rosseau got its name very early on as well. John Carthew made the first known reference to it under that name in 1835: Rousseau's Lake (the first ''u'' was later dropped). It's likely named for Jean Baptiste Rousseau, a Penetanguishene-based fur trader who operated in that part of the watershed. Some think that Rousseau himself named both that lake and Lake Joseph after his father. Coincidentally, when surveyor John Dennis ''rediscovered'' Lake Joseph in 1860, he named it Joseph too, after *his* father!

David Thompson had explored and mapped both lakes Rosseau and Joseph in 1837, but his maps and reports did not become known again until much later. He referred to both lakes as the Trading Lakes, due to evidence of fur-trading activity he saw there. Trading Lake, however, was the name more commonly applied to the second-largest lake in the Muskoka watershed, Lake of Bays.

Lake of Bays had a European name attached to it in 1826. It's labelled Lake Baptiste on Henry Briscoe's map of his historic ascent of the river that year. That name, its rationale unclear, didn't stick. Shortly afterwards Alexander Shirreff called the lake Trading Lake. He saw evidence of trading establishments there and said the lake appeared to have been long a principal station of the traders. Trading Lake it would officially remain for the rest of the 19th century. In the meantime, other names surfaced.

Although Frederick Baddeley didn't see Lake of Bays during his 1835 travels on the Muskoka River, his Indian guide knew of it and called it Lake Nagatoagoman (no translation given; Baddeley applied that name as well to the South Muskoka River). The most colourful name given to Lake of Bays comes from David Thompson's 1837 reports. According to Thompson, the Indians called it Nun ge low e nee goo mark so Lak a hagan (the Lake of the Forks from its many Deep Bays and Points of Land). Thompson himself called it Forked Lake and the Lake of the Two Bays. A glance at any map of the area confirms the suitability of all these names.

The modern name, Lake of Bays, was given in that form in 1853 by Alexander Murray during his explorations for the Geological Survey of Canada. It saw increasing use as the 19th century wore on and eventually replaced Trading Lake as the official name. The eastern bay of Lake of Bays at Dorset is still called Trading Bay.

Besides Lake of Bays, Alexander Murray gave names to six other major lakes in the Muskoka River watershed during his 1853 expedition, all of them still in use today. On the North Muskoka he named Mary Lake (after his oldest daughter), Fairy Lake (because of its beauty) and Peninsula Lake (due to its configuration); and on the Oxtongue River, Oxtongue Lake (shape), Canoe Lake (on account of having to stop there to build a new canoe) and Burnt Island Lake.

Oxtongue Lake had originally been named Cross Lake by David Thompson. Thompson also named a Canoe Lake further up the Oxtongue, for the same reason Murray did, however trappers later renamed it Tea Lake (trappers named many of the major headwater lakes in the 1860s and 1870s, as well as Ragged Falls and High Falls on the Oxtongue). Because Thompson's 1837 exploration records remained hidden for so many years, the names he gave to many lakes didn't come to light until after other names were already in common use.

A large lake virtually ignored by early explorers, because it wasn't on the principal canoe routes, was Hollow Lake east of Dorset. Deep, incredibly clear and ringed by high, wooded hills, it was called Kahweambejewagamog (the Lake of Many Echoes) by the Indians. Early settlers and trappers began calling it Hollow Lake, which carries the same connotations. For obvious reasons the latter persisted in popular usage, although official maps used the Indian name well into the 20th century. After the Second World War the name was officially changed to Kawagama Lake, this probably a corruption of Kahweambejewagamog. Many people still prefer to call it Hollow Lake.

Two other major lakes in the Muskoka watershed with interesting names are Skeleton Lake and Go Home Lake. Skeleton Lake got its name after a survey party discovered human skeletal remains on the north shore, probably in the 1860s. As the story goes, local settlers became interested and questioned a local Indian chief about these bones. He recounted a tale of an Indian mother who refused to abandon her dying son when the rest of her group broke camp and moved on. Both perished on the rocky, wind-swept shore.

Go Home is not only the name of a lake, but of a bay, a river and a waterfall nearby. It's clear how the name came about, but numerous people could plausibly have chosen it. Whether named by Indians, fur traders or lumbermen returning home after finishing their annual activities in the interior, or by the crews of Georgian Bay steamboats returning to their southern Georgian Bay ports, the Go Home area marked the beginning of the final stage of their journey.

One feature on the Muskoka River that particularly impressed all who saw it was South Falls on the South Branch. The highest on the river, in its natural state it ranked as one of the most spectacular scenes in central Ontario. It was the first, and for many years the only, waterfall on the river with a European name. Back in 1826 Henry Briscoe called it Sault du Sauvage (the Wild Falls). It so impressed surveyor Robert Bell in 1848 that he named it the Great Falls. That name, as well as the Grand Falls, persisted until the early 1860s. By then surveyors were referring to it as the South Falls, to distinguish it from the nearby large waterfall on the North Muskoka River, the North Falls. Today South Falls is still South Falls. The North Falls you will probably know better as Bracebridge Falls, as it has been known since 1864, when Bracebridge was named.

Entire books could be written about the origins of the names in the Muskoka River watershed — it would take a couple of volumes just to cover the hundreds of islands, bays and points in the Muskoka Lakes alone. Perhaps this brief account of the naming of the principal rivers, lakes and waterfalls will inspire some of you to investigate the names in your own corners of the district. It's a good way to learn about local history.

LUMBERING DAM, *Buck River at Campbell Falls. This basic design, simple and fast to erect of readily available materials, was typical of scores of lumbering dams in the watershed. Note the slide to carry logs. A government dam just upstream of this site now regulates the Buck River and Buck Lake.*

CHAPTER 6

Water on the Move: Controlling the Muskoka River

Sometimes it moves so slowly that its current is scarcely perceptible, only the silent, lazy rotation of a fallen leaf betraying any motion at all; at other times it swirls dramatically and dangerously, spilling from its channel onto the surrounding lands.

Up until the 1850s when virgin wilderness still covered all of the Muskoka watershed, and the river served only as a canoe route for Indian hunters and trappers, fur traders and explorers, the natural and often unpredictable rise and fall of water levels didn't seriously inconvenience anyone. But when settlement, lumbering, steamboat navigation and the construction of water-powered mills (and later hydroelectric stations) began to take place in the watershed, it became necessary to regulate the levels of lakes and the flow of water in streams to better accommodate these vital economic activities.

Today, with widespread cottage and residential development along the lakes and rivers of the Muskoka River system, and recreational use of the waterways at an all-time high, water regulation is essential to minimize flooding, protect fish spawning beds and maintain satisfactory boating conditions.

Deliberate control and management of the Muskoka River has a long history dating back to the late 1850s. We'll look at this important and interesting component of the Muskoka River story later in this chapter. Right now let's consider the natural factors that affect the flow of water through the rivers and lakes. From such knowledge comes a better understanding of why the river behaves as it does, of how it can be controlled, and of the limitations that have always affected its regulation and use.

RIVER RISING!

Even if we confine our comparisons to Ontario, the Muskoka is not a huge river. It's dwarfed by such major boundary waters as the St. Lawrence and Ottawa rivers, and the big rivers of the North which drain into James and Hudson bays. Nonetheless, the flow of water from the Muskoka River system exceeds that of such notable southern Ontario rivers as the Thames, the Grand and the Severn. Of the 30 rivers draining off the southern Ontario land mass, only the Trent and the Madawaska carry more water than the Muskoka.

In proportion to the surface area of its watershed, however, the Muskoka carries more water than any other major Ontario river. This of course has considerable implications, positive and negative, for water regulation and the use of the waterways.

The Muskoka carries so much water primarily because a greater depth of rain and snow falls on its watershed than on the watersheds of the other streams. Precipitation, ultimately, is the source of water flowing through any river system. Rain- and snowfall varies somewhat across the Muskoka watershed — highest in the west, declining eastward to the Algonquin Highland — but all parts receive plenty. Averaged out, about 1,000 millimetres (39.4 inches) of water lands on the watershed every year. Snowfall accounts for 30 percent of the annual precipitation, nearly three metres (10 feet) in its unmelted form.

Of course all that water has to go somewhere, and either directly over the land surface or indirectly through the ground, a good deal of it finds its way into creeks and rivers. Only about half of the precipitation falling on the Muskoka watershed actually reaches Georgian Bay. The rest evaporates from lakes, marshes and the soil, or transpires from the leaves of trees and other vegetation during the growing season. Still, a respectable 82 cubic metres (2,900 cubic feet) of water enters Georgian Bay every second, on average, from the Muskoka River system. The Musquash outlet handles about three quarters of the total discharge today. Virtually all the rest goes down the Moon, mostly in one wild rush in the spring.

The Muskoka River watershed's location is a big factor in the above-average amount of precipitation it receives. Sprawling up the western slope of the Algonquin Dome, it lies right in the path of the westerly winds that often blow in over Lake Huron and Georgian Bay. As these winds cross the open water they absorb extra moisture, particularly in the late fall and early winter, when the air is frequently colder than the water, and is warmed slightly by its passage over the lakes (the warmer the air, the more moisture it can hold).

When the moisture-laden winds reach the east shore of Georgian Bay, they're forced by the rising land surface to ascend. The air cools and the moisture condenses. In the winter the land may be cooler than the air; that also induces condensation of the water vapour. Either way, Muskoka residents scurry to find their umbrellas or their snow shovels.

The precipitation resulting from the winds coming in over Georgian Bay is in addition to that from normal weather systems that sprinkle southern Ontario more evenly. The phenomenon, called the *lake effect*, brings extra precipitation to the lee shores along other parts of the Great Lakes too. Lake-effect precipitation declines further inland and becomes nonexistent once you cross the height of land. In a *precipitation shadow* on the eastern slope of the Algonquin Dome, for instance, annual precipitation amounts to as much as 40 percent less than in the western part of the Muskoka River watershed.

The Muskoka watershed, like the rest of southern Ontario, experiences no pronounced wet or dry season. We do find some seasonal variation in Muskoka, but it's small compared to the extremes of precipitation characteristic of some climatic regions. Autumn and early winter in Muskoka tend to be the wettest, largely due to the lake effect, and late winter the driest (water in Georgian Bay and Lake Huron has cooled down or even frozen over by that time, cutting off the major source of moisture). Of course, wetter or drier than normal conditions can occur in any season, on a random basis according to weather patterns.

The flow of water in the Muskoka River, on the other hand, shows a marked seasonal variation: very high flows in the spring, much-diminished flows in the summer. The melting of the winter snows, of course, causes the high

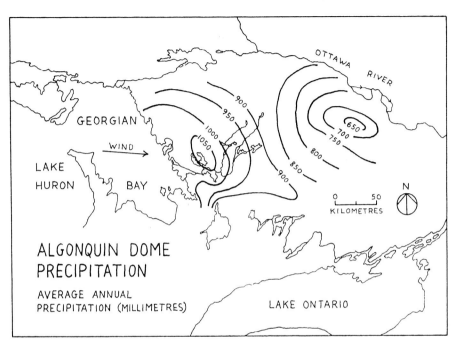

ALGONQUIN DOME PRECIPITATION

AVERAGE ANNUAL
PRECIPITATION (MILLIMETRES)

The isohyets (lines of equal precipitation) on this map clearly illustrate the high amount of precipitation on the Muskoka watershed, largely due to the lake effect, and the precipitation shadow on the eastern side of the Algonquin Dome.

Generous precipitation throughout the year contrasts sharply with a huge variation in stream flow. Small streams in the watershed often fluctuate even more widely, in some cases drying up completely in the summer. Beatrice is located 50 kilometres (31 miles) inland from Georgian Bay (between Bracebridge and Three Mile Lake) — still close enough, however, to feel the brunt of the lake effect.

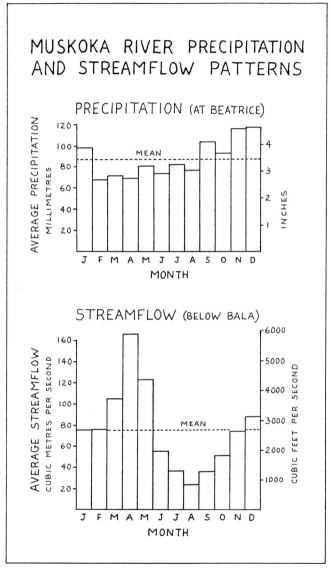

spring flows (the spring *freshet*) viewed with trepidation by those living on low-lying areas along lakes and streams. The magnitude and duration of the freshet depends on several uncontrollable factors: the amount of water lying on the watershed in the form of snow; how quickly the snow melts; the amount of rain during the run-off period; and ground conditions (dry, unfrozen ground can absorb some of the water, while frozen or saturated conditions cause rapid run-off into the streams and lakes).

High water conditions are not necessarily confined to the spring. Heavy rains in the summer (when lakes are already full for recreation and boating) or autumn can cause flooding during those seasons as well. So far, though, the worst floods on the Muskoka River have been in the spring. Since regular water-flow measurements were begun on the river in 1914, the worst watershed-wide flooding took place in the spring of 1928. Discharge rose to five times the average flow on the South Muskoka and into the Moon and Musquash, ten times the average on the North Muskoka. Flooding of the same order of magnitude occurred during the spring freshet of 1985, when the sudden onset of exceptionally mild weather caused a rapid snow melt.

Floods of that size, and many lesser ones, greatly exceed the capacity of stream channels to carry the water and of the lakes to store it. Streams excavate their channels wide and deep enough to comfortably handle only average conditions. Thus, when flows exceed a certain threshold, streams and often lakes overflow onto adjacent low-lying areas. These low areas, called *flood plains*, rightfully belong to the domain of the river. The natural inundation of flood plains would not cause problems if we humans could break our bad habit of building homes, cottages and roads on them.

It is during the spring freshet and other times of high stream flows that the Muskoka and other rivers do most of their erosion and deposition. The great energy of large volumes of fast-moving water allows streams to undercut their banks, dig into their beds and move the eroded materials downstream. Larger particles — sand, stones, even boulders — may just be deposited a little further down the channel; fine sands, silts and clays may carry right out into lakes where, as the current slows and loses energy, they settle to the bottom and often accumulate to form deltas.

Although the Muskoka River has produced notable floods over the years, none of them matched the destructive floods common in other watersheds, especially further south. For those whose access roads, yards and basements are periodically inundated, the Muskoka River floods must seem serious enough, but we don't suffer the multi-million-dollar damage and even loss of life caused by the inundation of entire communities and wide areas of land.

Several factors account for the comparatively mild flooding experienced on the Muskoka River. The land often rises quite abruptly away from the streams and lakes, and the deep channels of many of the major streams can carry substantial flows before they top their banks. Important too are the ways in which the watershed encourages or discourages the fast run-off of water into the streams and through the system. The steep, rocky nature of the terrain promotes speedy run-off, but the large number of lakes and the high proportion of forested land in the watershed more than compensate for that — most of the time.

Lakes (and marshes and swamps, too) act as natural water-storage reservoirs. They rise during periods of high inflow, then release the water gradually over an extended period.

With its large surface area a lake can handle much more water than a river channel before it begins to flood its shore-line. This effect is significant in the Muskoka watershed, where lakes cover nearly a seventh of the total area. A dam built at the outlet of a lake can be operated to achieve water-flow regulation beyond that which would occur naturally. This, in fact, is the basis of water management in the Muskoka River system.

It's worth noting that those tributaries of the Muskoka River with a below-average proportion of lake surface area — the Big East immediately comes to mind — suffer the greatest extremes of flow. A shallow channel, broad flood plain and steep, rocky headwater regions compound the flooding problems on the Big East.

Forests have a regulatory effect on water flows similar to that of lakes. The carpet of leaves and decaying vegetation that accumulates on the forest floor acts as a giant sponge, soaking up excess water, allowing it to percolate into the ground and then seep into the waterways at a more moderate rate. Some of the destructive floods on rivers to the south of Muskoka have been partly a result of cutting the forests to create farmland.

Lakes and forests not only help keep water flows from rising too high, but by permitting a more gradual release of water help keep them from falling too low in the summer. Nonetheless, in a dry summer even the large streams of the Muskoka system can experience flows less than ten percent of average. The practice of holding lake levels up in the summer for navigation and recreation rather than releasing the stored water sometimes exacerbates low stream flows during that season. Excessively low flows can interfere with hydroelectric generation, water supply and waste disposal.

Even when precipitation is normal, stream flows decline naturally in the summer due to the increased evaporation and transpiration during those warm months. For instance, during August (the month of lowest water flow on the Muskoka River) the long-term average flow of water into the Moon River from Lake Muskoka is 70 percent below the average annual flow, yet August precipitation is only slightly below average monthly precipitation. Artificial regulation cannot account for all of that great disparity.

During extended droughts virtually all of the flow in the Muskoka River comes from water stored in its lakes, ponds and marshes. Because of its rocky nature and thin soils, the watershed does not boast a large ground-water storage capacity to augment flows for long periods when there is no recharge from rain. Thick deposits of sand and gravel laid down by glacial meltwaters make excellent ground-water reservoirs; such deposits, however, actually cover a relatively small proportion of the Muskoka watershed.

The important role of forests has already been noted for the natural regulation of water flows. Forests also benefit streams by providing shade and reducing soil erosion, thereby keeping waters cool and clean. The Muskoka watershed is well wooded today, but back in the early days of settlement it must have seemed as though the virgin forests would fall to the homesteaders' and lumbermen's axes as they had further south. Concern about the destruction of the forests and the potential impact on the Muskoka and other rivers draining off the Algonquin Dome helped prompt the Ontario government to establish Algonquin Provincial Park in 1893. Straddling the Algonquin Highland, the park protected the headwaters of the Muskoka, Madawaska, Bonnechere, Petawawa and Amable du Fond rivers by keeping out the settlers and to some extent controlling the lumbermen.

As it turned out, the lumbermen and settlers threatened the forests in the rest of the Muskoka watershed only briefly. The wasteful and destructive logging practices of the first few decades gave way to more responsible timber harvesting and management philosophies, and the thin, infertile soils of the Shield quickly caused many settlers to abandon their hard-won fields. New forests reclaimed the denuded lands.

Even with the natural regulatory effects of the forests and lakes, water levels and flows in the Muskoka River system fluctuated in ways inconvenient to many potential users of the waterways. It was therefore necessary to install a network of dams on the lakes to bring the river under a greater degree of control.

WATER OVER THE DAM

As soon as settlement and more intense resource exploitation began in the Muskoka watershed, the various users of the water and the waterways began building their own dams to control the river to suit their needs. As development in the watershed and demands on the river system increased, that original independent and unco-ordinated network of privately operated dams gradually gave way to an expanded and more formalized system of water regulation which came under the control of the Ontario Department of Public Works. Today the Ministry of Natural Resources carries on this tradition of government management of the Muskoka River.

The lumbermen were among the first to begin regulating the Muskoka River. They needed an assured supply of water to float their logs down the creeks and rivers to Georgian Bay and later to sawmills within the watershed. The spring freshet and natural flows could not always meet their needs. So, after they began logging in the Muskoka watershed in the 1850s, the lumbermen built hundreds of timber dams that stored water for the log drives by raising the levels of existing lakes and even creating a few new ones. Most, though not all, of these dams were erected in headwater areas or on the smaller streams, where the greatest danger of insufficient water existed. They also built dams on the larger Hollow, Oxtongue, Big East and Buck rivers, and one on the Moon that effected an early diversion of waters into the Musquash.

The operators of water-powered sawmills and grist mills also built a number of early dams, mainly in the 1860s and 1870s. On smaller streams these regulated the levels of small lakes or artificial mill ponds to provide an adequate flow to the waterwheel or turbine during working hours. On larger streams and rivers where the natural flow was always adequate, mill dams served merely to raise the head of water and divert some of the flow into the mill race. A few of these coincidentally controlled the levels of major lakes. The first dams on Mary Lake (1869), Fairy Lake (1873) and Lake of Bays (1872) were all mill dams. These also served the lumbermen during their log drives.

The advent of steamboat navigation on the big lakes of the Muskoka River system in the 1860s and 1870s made it essential to maintain adequate and reasonably stable water levels on these lakes during the navigation season. Out of that necessity the Department of Public Works first became involved in the construction and operation of dams on the Muskoka River. Not surprisingly the first Public Works dam

LUMBERING DAM AND SLIDE, Musquash River. *This 1889 photograph illustrates a more refined construction of squared-timber cribs commonly used for all major Muskoka River dams, government and private, until stone masonry and then concrete became the preferred materials in the 20th century.* · Archives of Ontario Acc. 9912-I-38

was built on Lake Muskoka, the largest and most important lake in the watershed, and the first to have steamers running on it.

Under natural conditions the level of Lake Muskoka could fall as much as 2.7 metres (9 feet) between late spring and autumn. Such a variation made navigation very risky: a channel perfectly safe in June might be full of treacherous shoals by September. Around 1870 a mill owner built a small dam on one of the outlets of Lake Muskoka at Bala; however, it did not affect the lake level to any great degree. In 1873 the Public Works began constructing a control dam on the main outlet channel.

The new dam was intended to prevent water levels from falling too far in the summer, while at the same time enlargement of the channel by blasting would allow water to leave more quickly in the spring, thus limiting the rise in the lake level. Excavation of rock ledges obstructing the flow of water into a southern outlet channel necessitated the construction of a second dam there in 1878. Both Bala dams have been rebuilt or replaced several times since.

The Department of Public Works also built dams on the other lakes where steamers operated. Those on Mary Lake (1876), Fairy Lake (1877 — this one, at the Huntsville Lock, also controlled Lake Vernon and later Peninsula Lake, too) and Lake of Bays (1918) replaced dams built earlier by mill owners. A dam on the Indian River near the Port Carling Lock (1882) was the first one on that site, built to regulate the levels of Lake Rosseau and Lake Joseph.

All of these Public Works dams served other needs besides maintenance of navigation water levels. Some continued to function as mill dams, and all were used for flood control, water conservation and log drives. Such multiple use

virtually demanded that they be controlled by a central agency, in this case the government of Ontario, to insure that all users of the waterways be served as well as possible. Left to their own devices, the lumber companies for instance might draw too much water out of the lakes for their log drives, thus adversely affecting navigation and possibly mill operation.

Starting in the early 1900s the Muskoka River became increasingly important as a source of hydroelectricity. That meant that substantial stream flows had to be maintained even in times of drought to spin the hydroelectric turbines, which gulped far greater quantities of water than the old mills. This was particularly critical because until the 1950s the Muskoka River power stations supplied practically all of Muskoka's electricity, as well as significant amounts for towns to the south.

To provide for power generation it was necessary to store large quantities of water from the spring freshet for use later on in the summer. The Public Works dams on the big lakes could serve this purpose only to a limited degree, due to the necessity of maintaining navigation levels. Much of the water stored in those lakes became available for power production only in the autumn and winter. Reservoirs impounded behind the dams at some of the hydroelectric stations themselves provided water storage sufficient only to handle daily fluctuations in the demand for electricity.

Consequently, attention turned to the headwater lakes of the Hollow, Oxtongue and Big East rivers. The lumber companies had dammed most of these years before, but with lumbering on the decline by this time these dams were not needed so much for log drives. Between the world wars — the period of the greatest expansion of hydroelectric generation on the Muskoka River — the Department of Public Works rebuilt or replaced many of those old lumbering dams to conserve spring run-off. These included the dams on Tea, Joe, Burnt Island and Ragged lakes in the Oxtongue headwaters, and on Tasso, Camp and McCraney lakes in the Big East watershed. On the Hollow River Ontario Hydro built a big new dam on Hollow (Kawagama) Lake in 1925-26, this also the site of an old lumbering dam. The Department of Public Works later took over the new dam.

In 1940, in an effort to achieve better overall management of the Muskoka River system, the Department of Public Works and Ontario Hydro signed the Hackner-Holden Agreement. It specified how several major lakes in the watershed should be regulated, primarily to provide adequate river flows for hydroelectric generation, but also to protect fish spawning beds and serve navigation and flood-control needs.

Since the Second World War the relative importance of the Muskoka River for power production has greatly declined as new transmission lines made available abundant supplies of electricity from other parts of Ontario. In addition, the post-war years have seen a tremendous growth in cottage development and recreational activity on lakes and rivers throughout the watershed.

Water management practices reflected these changes. The Department of Public Works built dams (or replaced old ones) on several previously undeveloped lakes where cottages sprang up — for example, on Go Home, Fletcher and Livingstone lakes. Some of these dams functioned solely to maintain the lake levels for recreation. In 1969 the Hackner-Holden Agreement was revised to favour maintenance of summer recreation water levels on the major Muskoka River lakes, at the expense of certain draw-downs originally

designed to provide extra water for power stations. A master plan subsequently adopted for Algonquin Park placed severe restrictions on the summer draw-downs permitted on headwater lakes within the park — again, in the interests of recreation. For many years water stored in these lakes had been used to augment stream flows and lake levels lower down in the watershed during the summer.

Water regulation on the Muskoka River must take into account certain ecological concerns, the moist crucial being the protection of fish spawning beds. For instance, when lake levels are drawn down in the autumn and winter, following the end of the summer recreation and navigation season, care must be taken not to jeopardize the lake trout spawn. Because the trout lay their eggs in fairly shallow water during October, the draw-down must be restricted between then and late winter, when the eggs hatch.

Over on the Moon River the annual spring pickerel (walleye) spawn below Moon Falls depends on the maintenance of an adequate stream flow for the duration of the spawning and hatching period. Sometimes Ontario Hydro must cut back power production at its Musquash River hydroelectric plants and allow the water to go down the Moon River instead. That can happen if the spring freshet, which normally fills both rivers, doesn't last long enough.

Flood control has long been a major objective of water management, and an important function of the Muskoka River dams and the storage capacity of the lakes behind them. This has become more crucial with the great increase in shoreline development in the watershed. Control of the spring freshet is achieved, or attempted, by drawing lake levels down through the autumn and winter to provide storage space to hold part of the freshet, ideally enough of it to pre-

MOON RIVER DAM. This Ontario Hydro diversion dam, built in 1937-38, *normally blocks the Moon River, allowing the water to flow down the Musquash River instead. An earlier lumbering dam effected a similar diversion to aid log drives on the Musquash.*

vent excessively high water flows on the rivers without the lakes themselves rising too high. However, even though dams can regulate some 450 square kilometres (174 square miles) of lakes to provide storage, the vast amounts of water than can enter the river from snow melt and spring rains sometimes exceeds the capacity of the lakes to store it, and flooding does occur.

The attainment of the relatively high summer lake levels for recreation and boating depends on adequate refilling during the freshet, sometimes a problem in a dry spring. The maintenance of these levels through the summer can be a problem too, if rainfall is below normal, due to the normally low inflow and high evaporation during that season. Since it isn't desirable to cut off the outflow into the rivers completely, lake levels will slowly fall during a dry summer.

There is a potential danger inherent in the high summer lake levels desired by cottagers and boaters in the Muskoka River watershed: relatively little extra storage capacity exists to absorb severe rainstorms that sometimes hit the area. These can be reliably predicted only a day or so in advance. Unfortunately, the size of the Muskoka watershed and the amount of water contained in it means that it takes about two weeks to discharge enough water to lower the lake levels significantly. Thus, from time to time a summer flood strikes the river.

It's not easy to regulate water levels and stream flows to satisfy all needs in a watershed like that of the Muskoka. The numerous conflicting demands upon the waterways, the large and sometimes unpredictable amounts of water that can pass through the system, the variety of factors that affect run-off, the complex network of lakes and streams, all with different capacities for storing or carrying water, the time lag brought on by the size of the watershed — all of this affects water management decisions.

And as the term *system* implies, the impact of an occurrence in one part of the watershed — for instance, a large input of water from a localized storm or the opening of a dam — has a ripple effect (or a flood effect!) down through all the other lakes and connecting streams. This means that dozens of other dams have to be adjusted, in a co-ordinated fashion, to maintain water conditions within desirable limits.

The responsibility of regulating the Muskoka River belongs to the water management staff of the Ontario Ministry of Natural Resources in Huntsville (the M.N.R. absorbed the Department of Public Works in the early 1970s). The M.N.R. now owns some 32 dams in the Muskoka River watershed. About 18 of these, controlling most of the major lakes, are important for flood control and water conservation purposes. The rest serve mainly to hold recreation water levels. Some of the latter have little or no provision for active regulation.

The water-management staff regulate lake levels and stream flows on the Muskoka River by manipulating the stop-logs (or control valves, in some instances) in the various dams. They base their operational decisions on a thorough knowledge and understanding of how the Muskoka River system behaves under a variety of conditions, and on the interpretation of data received from gauges throughout the watershed which monitor lake levels, stream flows and precipitation. Some of these gauges, including several in remote areas, operate automatically, transmitting the data over telephone lines or via satellite. During the critical period leading up to the spring freshet, water-management staff measure the water content of the snow lying on the watershed and determine the ground conditions underneath.

BAYSVILLE DAM, *South Muskoka River.* Dams on this strategic site date back to 1872, but the gracefully curving concrete structure you see today was built in 1959-60 by the Public Works Department. Regulating Lake of Bays, it is one of the more important control dams in the Muskoka River system.

DISTRESS DAM, *Big East River.* A lumbering dam built on this site in the 1880s created an artificial lake, Distress Pond, to hold water for log drives. The present concrete dam, built in 1955 by the Department of Public Works, maintains the pond for recreation.

Flood forecasting for the Muskoka River — indeed, for all Ontario rivers — is handled by the M.N.R.'s Streamflow Forecast Centre in Toronto. The centre receives water data from the various watersheds across the province and constantly monitors and interprets weather information. It seeks to provide as much advance warning as possible of flooding on any of the rivers, or of impending weather conditions that might lead to flooding — heavy rains, for instance, or hot temperatures that could cause a quick snow melt. Information and warnings from the Centre pertaining to the Muskoka River go to the water-management staff in Huntsville, who then act accordingly.

The most frequent and serious flooding in the Muskoka watershed takes place on the lower Big East near Huntsville. The local water-management staff can now give adequate advance warning of high water to flood-plain residents based on information received from automatic gauges further up the river.

In the early 1980s several moderately serious floods on the Big East and other parts of the river system solidified a growing dissatisfaction among some people in the watershed about how the Muskoka River was being managed and sparked demands for changes (the floods, it should be mentioned, were due to natural, uncontrollable factors). As a result, in 1983-84 the M.N.R. and Environment Canada jointly sponsored a water-management improvement study which examined all aspects of water management, waterway use and public concerns in the Muskoka River watershed.

In the end it was found that the existing water-management system was basically sound, requiring only some fine-tuning here and there to alleviate particular concerns. Much of the dissatisfaction had stemmed not from operational shortcomings but from lack of public understanding of the nature of the river system.

We must remember that despite all the control dams designed to regulate water levels and flows, the Muskoka River nonetheless still possesses a built-in natural propensity for inconvenient or even damaging behaviour. We can use the river to serve our needs, but we must also respect it as a natural force of the planet.

SOUTH FALLS. *The spectacular upper chutes of South Falls crash down a narrow chasm below the tiny and frail-looking Muskoka Road bridge in the 1870s. Highway 11 now crosses here.*

- drawing by Seymour Penson in the Guide Book and Atlas of Muskoka and Parry Sound Districts, 1879

CHAPTER 7

Tumbling Waters: The Story of the Muskoka River Waterfalls

Nature bestows upon us few spectacles so dynamic and inspiring as waterfalls. No other natural feature enjoys such universal popularity as a scenic attraction. The thundering cataract pounding into a mist-filled gorge, the gentle chute gliding almost soundlessly over time-worn rock, the feathery cascade weaving down a wooded glen, each captivates the imagination in its own unique way. Waterfalls appeal to all of our senses — that is the secret of their magic. We not only see the plummeting waters and the eroded rocks, but we hear the roar, feel the tingle of spray on our cheeks or the vibrations underfoot, savour the clean, sharp smell of wet rocks and moss.

The Muskoka River and its tributaries leap, tumble and slide over hundreds of beautiful waterfalls that have long been a source of enjoyment to all those who have visited them. To be sure, none of them matches the awesome size and world-wide fame of a Niagara, but set amongst the rough grey rock and towering pines of the Canadian Shield, they frequently possess a primitive grandeur that makes them just as appealing. Along with the lakes, forests and hills, they're an integral part of the character and scenery of Muskoka.

Not only notable for their scenic qualities, the Muskoka River waterfalls have played important roles in the settlement and economy of the district. Several towns and hamlets owe their locations and existence at least in part to waterfalls and rapids that provided mill sites, convenient points for bridges, or created a head of navigation. Bracebridge, Port Sydney, Hoodstown, Muskoka Falls, Matthiasville, Baysville, Dee Bank, Port Carling and Bala all qualify for that distinction.

Probably the most important contribution of the waterfalls has been water power. The earliest manufacturing establishments in Muskoka, the sawmills and grist mills so vital to the pioneers, depended on the free, readily harnessed energy of the falls. Later that energy was tapped to spin the generators in hydroelectric stations which for many years provided most of Muskoka's electricity and substantial quantities for towns and cities further south. These stations still generate enough electricity to supply 12,000 homes.

The waterfalls on the river also had negative impacts. Foremost, they blocked otherwise navigable waterways and contributed to the failure of early investigations to determine if the Muskoka River might provide a link in a proposed canal between Georgian Bay and the Ottawa River. During the more than 80 years that the lumbermen used the river to float logs down to the sawmills or to Georgian Bay, the waterfalls presented difficult, though not insurmountable obstacles. Logjams in the narrow constrictions and extensive damage to the timber as it crashed down over the rocks were a constant aggravation to the lumber companies.

One of the most interesting chapters in the story of the Muskoka River waterfalls deals with the circumstances of their nature and existence: their origins, evolution and eventual extinction.

THE GIANT STAIRCASE

From its highest sources on the Algonquin Highland the Muskoka River descends some 400 metres (1,312 feet) to its mouths on Georgian Bay. That's a very modest drop compared with streams in mountainous regions, but when you consider that for most of its length the river passes through lakes or flows in nearly level channels, you begin to appreciate the tremendous scope that must exist for waterfalls.

Like the Muskoka River itself, the waterfalls on the river owe their origins to the glaciers of the Ice Age, the last of which melted back from the Muskoka watershed just over 11,000 years ago. The pre-glacial ancestor of the Muskoka, you may recall from Chapter 3, flowed swiftly but more or less evenly down the slope of the Algonquin Dome, as though rushing down a giant ramp. No waterfalls of any significance interrupted its course.

When the glaciers advanced southward over the watershed, they scraped and scoured the land, deepening the valleys and digging thousands of basins in the bedrock. After the ice retreated, the new streams that began flowing across the land — the fledgling Muskoka River system — descended step-like from basin to basin like a giant staircase. Waterfalls sprang to life as the water spilled over the steep, rocky barriers between the basins. In between, across the flat "treads" of the staircase, the water flowed through lakes that filled many of the basins, or carved placid channels in the

gravel, sand and clay that glacial meltwaters and subsequent run-off had deposited in the rest. In many instances, so thick were these surficial deposits that it took decades, even centuries for the streams to uncover the bedrock barriers between the basins and form waterfalls.

The locations and physical characteristics of the Muskoka River waterfalls are intimately related to the bedrock geology of the watershed. Each waterfall exists at a point where a stream spills over ledges or outcrops of rock that are harder or more structurally sound than the rock immediately around. These resistant outcrops better withstood the ravages of weathering and erosion over the ages, and the scouring by the glaciers. They now stand up as barriers to the streams' progress, natural dams between the bedrock basins scooped out on each side.

With few exceptions these resistant barriers are composed of gneiss, the predominant rock in the watershed. This hard crystalline metamorphic rock is characterized by a marked banded or layered appearance. The bands are generally tilted. Ancient rivers and glaciers exposed and eroded the softer and weaker bands, the result being a series of parallel ridges or lines of hills capped by the harder bands, alternating with valleys and troughs eroded into the weaker ones. Along the floors of these valleys the glaciers gouged chains of basins separated by constrictions where harder or sounder layers predominated.

When a stream flows along one of these erosion valleys — commonly the case in the Muskoka watershed — waterfalls tumble through the constrictions. They're usually long, slanting chutes rushing down V-shaped troughs eroded into the tilted gneiss layers. Notable examples of this type of waterfall include the Hogs Trough on the Oxtongue River,

THE HOGS' TROUGH, Oxtongue Rapids, Oxtongue River. *Here you see a classic example of a chute rushing down a V-shaped trough eroded into tilted layers of bedrock gneiss. Many Muskoka River waterfalls display this configuration.*

the Long Slide chute on the Hollow, upper Bracebridge Falls, and Bala, Island, South Twin and Moon falls on the Moon River.

There are many instances, however, where streams flow at right angles to the ridge and valley terrain, following old fault lines or merely taking advantage of other natural low points. When this happens, waterfalls spill over the resistant crests of the ridges from a basin in one valley to another basin in the adjacent valley. These falls display a great variety of forms, depending on such factors as the soundness of the rock and its direction of tilt. They include broad, steep leaps over cliffs (best exemplified by High Falls and Wilson's Falls on the North Muskoka), energetic cascades bouncing down hillsides (common on smaller streams throughout the watershed), and narrow chutes boiling through clefts eroded into valley walls.

Some of the Muskoka River's largest and most spectacular waterfalls fit into the cleft category — Ragged Falls and High Falls on the Oxtongue, South Falls on the South Muskoka, and West Twin Falls on the Moon. The clefts are usually the result of erosion in heavily jointed rock. When the gneiss cooled after its formation a billion years ago, shrinkage caused a rectangular pattern of cracks (joints) to develop. Various slow weathering processes, and sometimes more dramatic events like faulting, further opened up the joints. The glaciers and subsequently the pounding water of the falls readily removed the loosened blocks of rock to excavate a cleft or chasm.

Very few of the Muskoka River waterfalls are actually true *falls*, that is, vertical plunges over a precipice, as at High Falls on the North Muskoka (and even there the water doesn't fall straight down). Such descents, when they do occur, make up

only a part of the total height. Due to the hardness of even the less resistant layers of gneiss, the water does not readily undercut the harder capping layers. As a result we don't find the sort of free-fall drops characteristic of Niagara and other waterfalls where easily eroded sedimentary rock layers make up part of the formation.

Most often on the Muskoka River the water slides or tumbles down ramp- or step-like inclines best described as *chutes*. On smaller streams especially we find cascades, series of small falls, chutes and short, steep rapids. *Rapids*, shallow turbulent reaches of swift water, occur quite commonly where streams have not yet been able to remove thick accumulations of stones or boulders from their channels, or where they flow over suitably sloped bedrock. The stones are usually of glacial origin; at the foot of waterfalls they're often the result of more recent excavation of a cleft by the falls itself.

Although the configuration of the rock formations largely determines the general appearance and dimensions of waterfalls, it is the falling water of course that actually brings them to life by generating the sights, sounds and sensations that so delight us. Ironically that same falling water eventually destroys the falls.

Falling water represents an enormous concentration of energy expenditure. Aided by abrasive grit carried in the water, that energy goes to work on the rock, slowly scouring and pounding it away until it no longer impedes the stream channel. In the long and constantly evolving lives of streams, waterfalls exist as temporary features, brief interruptions of youthful exuberance. By erosion of the steep points and deposition on the flats and in the lakes, streams smooth out their gradients as they age.

NIAGARA OF THE NORTH, High Falls, North Muskoka River. This impressive cataract roars over a resistant ridge of tilted gneiss layers, plunging down a cliff into a trough or basin eroded into the slightly weaker underlying layers.

HIGH FALLS, Oxtongue River. A tranquil scene with dramatic geology. Note the cleft eroded into the cliff and the well-defined layered structure of the gneiss. Many maps erroneously call this Gravel Falls.

The gneiss underlying the Muskoka River waterfalls is so hard that the natural self-destructive process will take hundreds of thousands of years to run its course. Already, though, you can see evidence of its progress: rock polished smooth as glass, potholes (circular erosion cavities ground out by stones whirling in plunging waters), and narrow clefts eroded into cliff faces. Some of the energy of the falling water dissipates in swirling currents at the foot of the falls. These currents scoop out easily eroded materials to create the oval *plunge pools* found at many Muskoka River waterfalls.

The energy of a waterfall varies directly with the volume of water going over it and the distance that water drops. It's often expressed as *power* — the rate of energy expenditure. We can rank waterfalls according to how powerful they are. In fact, we can equate power with magnitude: the largest waterfall will be the most powerful waterfall.

By far the most powerful waterfall in the Muskoka watershed is South Falls on the South Muskoka River. At the average river flow it represents nearly 9,000 kilowatts. Plunging 33.2 metres (109 feet) South Falls also happens to be the highest mainstream waterfall in the watershed. Bala Falls, at the outlet of Lake Muskoka, carries the greatest average flow of water, 75 cubic metres (2,550 cubic feet) per second, or nearly three times the amount that goes over South Falls. But due to its low height of just six metres (20 feet) it ranks only fourth in terms of power.

Energy or power has much more than just geological or statistical significance. It can be harnessed using waterwheels or hydraulic turbines to drive mill machinery or spin electric generators. Chapters 8 and 9 deal with the important contribution the power of the Muskoka River waterfalls made to industry and life in the district.

THE GREATEST FALLS · AND SOME MERELY BEAUTIFUL

To the Indians, fur traders, explorers and other early travellers who used the Muskoka River as a canoe route, the scores of waterfalls along the way must have been a mixed blessing. Each waterfall meant yet another portage, sometimes a long, arduous one. On the other hand, even as they sweated and toiled up the portage trails bent under the weight of pack and canoe, those early travellers must certainly have been moved by the wild beauty of waters thundering over ancient rocks between stands of giant virgin pine.

We know from diaries and reports that one waterfall on the Muskoka River impressed those who saw it more so than any other: the Great Falls, so named in 1848 by surveyor Robert Bell. Situated on the South Muskoka River at the present Highway 11 crossing, it was the highest, wildest and most powerful waterfall in the Muskoka watershed, a truly awesome spectacle unmatched in the mid-Ontario wilderness.

Ambling peacefully between low wooded hills, the South Muskoka suddenly and unexpectedly poured into a great rift, an 850-metre-long (½-mile) crack, probably an old fault, that ripped through the Precambrian gneiss beneath the forest. In quick succession the water rushed over a pair of comparatively modest chutes into swirling pools, then it burst into a narrow chasm and rampaged over a series of spectacular falls, the thundering mass of water pulverized to whiteness by the jagged rocks, the mist and spray rising like clouds between the dark chasm walls and the luxuriant tangle of cedar, pine and hemlock clinging to the precipitous slopes. At the bottom the violence ended in a tiny pool dwarfed by a towering cliff and the high valley walls.

SOUTH FALLS. *Near the bottom of its tumultuous descent the water boils through this incredibly narrow cleft only a few metres wide. An ancient fault probably initiated the wound that is now the South Falls gorge.*

Of the total descent 43 metres (141 feet) through the Great Falls rift, nearly three quarters occurred in that final awesome gorge. That 300-metre (984-foot) section became known in the early 1860s as South Falls (because it was on the South Muskoka). Settlers began to call the smaller upper chutes the Hanna Chutes, after the Richard Hanna family. In 1862 the Hannas were among the first to settle at the Great Falls on the site of Muskoka Falls village.

The Great Falls seemed almost like a magnet during the years leading up to the beginnings of settlement in Muskoka. As settlement began it was chosen as the crossing point for the Muskoka colonization road, as the western terminus of the Peterson Road, and, as Robert Bell had first suggested in 1848, as the site for a town. The unrivalled beauty and tremendous water power of the falls, combined with a central location accessible by both road and water, made many people think Muskokaville (or Muskoka Falls, as the settlement was called) would become an important centre. These hopes didn't materialize; nearby Bracebridge quickly assumed the dominant position in the area.

For a number of years the Great Falls remained an unharnessed natural wonder, loved by the tourists flocking to Muskoka in increasing numbers, loathed by the lumbermen who had to drive their logs over it. A big log slide constructed around South Falls in 1878-79 solved the woes of the lumbermen.

After the turn of the century the Great Falls finally achieved the economic importance earlier denied it, when it was harnessed to generate electricity for Muskoka and regions to the south. But the hydroelectric stations, one at South Falls and another at the Hanna Chutes, irrevocably altered Muskoka's most magnificent cataract. Modern highway bridges further imposed upon the scene. Yet despite all these changes the Great Falls is still capable of putting on an inspiring display of fury reminiscent of its original wild splendour.

Not far from the Great Falls, near the mouth of the North Muskoka River, tumbled another scenic waterfall, one known in the early 1860s as the North Falls. Scarcely one third as high as the Great Falls and almost serene by comparison, it succeeded where the Great Falls had failed at sparking an important settlement. It was chosen as the North Muskoka River crossing point for the Muskoka Road and boasted natural advantages similar to those of the Great Falls. However, flanked by less intimidating terrain, its water power was quickly harnessed for mills that provided a potent nucleus for a frontier community — a community named Bracebridge in 1864. The falls was also much closer by water to Lake Muskoka than the Great Falls, and its larger plunge pool provided a fine harbour: thus Bracebridge became the eastern port of call for A.P. Cockburn's steamboats starting in 1866. As an important distribution and supply point, Bracebridge grew even faster, while Muskoka Falls village remained just a small rural hamlet.

Bracebridge Falls continued to be an important asset to the community. A water-powered woollen mill that opened on its bank became one of the town's leading industries. The falls was also the site of the first hydroelectric development in Muskoka and helped make Bracebridge the Ontario pioneer in municipal hydroelectric generation. Today it still serves the town as a source of electricity, in addition to providing a scenic focal point and a lasting reminder of the town's interesting past.

In its natural state Bracebridge Falls was one of the pretti-

BRACEBRIDGE FALLS TODAY. *Thousands of visitors view this scenic waterfall every summer and autumn, but not so many see it roaring at the height of the spring freshet. The upper part of the falls isn't visible from this vantage point.*

THE NORTH FALLS, *(Bracebridge Falls)*. *In the 1870s only the original Bird Woollen Mill and the Muskoka Road bridge existed along the upper two thirds of the falls. The lane on the right, Mill Street, led to the sawmill and grist mill at the bottom.*

· woodcut originally in The Globe and Canada Farmer, *Toronto, 1879*

NORTH FALLS, BRACEBRIDGE.
(From a photograph by John Hollingworth Beatrice, Muskoka.)

est on the river. The water rushed unchecked down a 200-metre (656-foot) chute lined with pine, cedar and birch, the lovely oval pool at the bottom reflected unbroken forest climbing the steep hills all around. Of course, the felling of the trees and the proliferation of mills, dams, bridges and other development that accompanied settlement changed all that. Over the years, though, the raw frontier scene mellowed; today the 16-metre-high (52-foot) falls displays a pleasing harmony between the natural and the man-made, a harmony perhaps best exemplified by the rustic stone powerhouse that seems to grow right out of the rock beside the tumbling waters at the bottom. Walkways and historical plaques allow the visitor to soak up some of the history of the falls as well as to enjoy its scenic attributes.

Not far upstream from Bracebridge the North Muskoka River plunges over two more large waterfalls. These falls still retain much of their original primitive beauty. The closest, 12.5-metre-high (41-foot) Wilson's Falls, doesn't draw the attention it deserves, despite its splendid scenery and proximity to Bracebridge. In a section of valley filled with rock and pine, the North Muskoka rolls out of the forest and pours over the brow of a wide, low cliff. At the height of the spring freshet the cataract spreads out across the entire 100-metre (328-foot) breadth of this rock face to form a thundering wall of white framed between majestic stands of pine.

Wilson's Falls is named for Gilman Wilson, who co-founded a water-powered sawmill there in the 1860s. Later the town of Bracebridge built a small hydroelectric station on the old mill site. Its generator still hums away inside the quaint red-brick powerhouse. The configuration of Wilson's Falls allowed its power to be tapped without seriously affecting its wild character.

The existence of a public picnic grounds beside it, just off busy Highway 11, has contributed to the much greater popularity of High Falls. Its abrupt, nearly vertical plunge 14.6 metres (48 feet) down a cliff into a huge oval pool surrounded by pine forests makes it one of Muskoka's premier natural attractions. Visit High Falls in the spring if you can. Swollen by meltwaters, the twin southern cataracts put on a spellbinding display that makes you think of Niagara. A third, northern cataract of High Falls that once tumbled down a narrow chute in the cliff is the inconspicuous location of another small hydroelectric development.

On the South Muskoka River the only really large waterfall upstream from the Great Falls is the next one, 10.7-metre-high (35-foot) Trethewey Falls. Bouncing down the face of a pine-clad ridge, this long set of rapids and low chutes was dammed halfway up to supply a hydroelectric station and, like the other Muskoka River waterfalls so harnessed, often has most of its flow diverted to the turbine in the summer. Nonetheless, Trethewey Falls still makes a worthwhile destination for the sightseer. The falls is named for James Trethewey, who built a sawmill there about 1865.

Along their upper reaches both the North Muskoka and the South Muskoka spill over a number of picturesque little chutes and rapids. Some of these became important mill sites, and one, Matthias Falls on the South Muskoka, is now the site of a huge dam built to supply yet another hydroelectric station. If we continue upstream into the headwaters of both streams, up onto the Hollow, Oxtongue and Big East rivers, we again discover some large waterfalls, waterfalls notable not only for their size but for unrivalled natural beauty and largely unspoiled settings in those more remote eastern valleys.

WILSON'S FALLS, *North Muskoka River. A thundering wall of white framed between pine forests just minutes from downtown Bracebridge. You must visit it in the spring to see it in this splendid condition.*

LONG SLIDE CHUTE, *Hollow River. A bold, rocky ridge looms over these slanting cascades which were once by-passed by a 210-metre (689-foot) log slide. Autumn colours turn this into a scene of unparalleled beauty.*

RAGGED FALLS, Oxtongue River. Early trappers could hardly have chosen a more appropriate name for this rough, brawling cataract, captured here on film during the spring freshet by a rather drenched author.

Anyone familiar with the Dorset area may know of the scenic Long Slide chute on the Hollow River just east of the village. Here the incredibly clear, naturally greenish-tinted waters of the Hollow gush like a mountain stream over a series of slanting chutes between masses of steel-grey rock, then bubble and foam down a twisting, rocky rapids below. In the woods on the north side you can still see the remains of the big log slide that once by-passed the chute and part of the rapids below.

For the sheer size and beauty of its waterfalls the Oxtongue River is virtually unmatched in the Muskoka watershed. As it pours down off the Algonquin Highland it makes its highest and most impressive leap over 25-metre (82-foot) Ragged Falls. Brawling down a rough chasm excavated into the valley side, surrounded by unbroken forests of pine, hemlock and hardwoods, this wilderness wonder puts on a magnificent display of untamed splendour truly evocative of the Canadian Shield and of northern rivers. Although it's obviously most awesome when filled with raging spring meltwaters, Ragged Falls is an inspiring scene even in the summer, when much-diminished flows bare the shattered rock in the floor of the chasm. The Ministry of Natural Resources maintains a public viewing area at the site, off Highway 60 just east of Oxtongue Lake.

Not far upstream from Ragged Falls we find one of the most startlingly beautiful waterfalls in the entire Muskoka watershed. Early trappers called it High Falls, but it really deserves a more exotic name. Deep in the forested wilderness a tiny pool nestles in the shadow of a sheer cliff fringed with cedars, and lofty pines and hemlock. A cleft splits the rock face from top to bottom; down it the Oxtongue tumbles in a steep, shimmering cascade that ends in the smooth black waters of the little pool. A subtle interplay of light and shadow seems to intensify the elements of the scene. The atmosphere — secluded, serene, unspoiled — make you wish you could just sit by this falls forever.

Downriver from Ragged Falls, below Oxtongue Lake, the Oxtongue puts on its most sustained show of violence as it twists and turns down the treacherous Oxtongue Rapids. Spread out along five kilometres (3 miles) of wooded valley, gentle riffles murmur past stately hemlock groves, angry rapids boil through birch and maple forest, roaring chutes squeeze between walls of rock, with something new and exciting at every bend of the channel. Altogether the Oxtongue drops 43 metres (141 feet) over these scenic rapids. In one place it dashes through a narrow V-shaped gorge eroded into boldly exposed layers of tilted gneiss — the amazing Hogs Trough chute.

Further to the north, the upper Big East River plummets almost as steeply as the Oxtongue as it too bounces down off the Algonquin Highland. Long, stony rapids gurgling through the hills characterize most of its descent, but right below Distress Pond it cascades over the low cliffs and rock ledges of the Distress Chutes. These are not a single grand spectacle like a South Falls or a Ragged Falls, but rather a series of wild scenes that unfold as the water spills down through the forest along a twisting 600-metre (1,970-foot) course. Steeped in the remote uninhabited atmosphere that cloaks much of the upper Big East valley, the little-known Distress Chutes rank among the most scenic waterfalls in Muskoka.

Many of the Muskoka River's finest waterfalls, such as those on the Oxtongue and Big East, remained hidden from most early vacationers in Muskoka due to their remote locations. However, several smaller but no less scenic waterfalls closer to the big resort hotels on the Muskoka Lakes became popular destinations in the late 1800s, and continue to draw cottagers and vacationers from around those lakes today. These falls are found on the Rosseau, Skeleton and Dee rivers, all tributaries to Lake Rosseau.

By far the highest and most impressive of these falls is 19-metre-high (62-foot) Rosseau Falls right at the mouth of the Rosseau River. It practically dries up sometimes in the summer, but in the spring or after heavy rains it suddenly transforms into a thundering explosion of white water that carves a 250-metre-long (820-foot) path of violence between forests of maple, oak and pine sweeping down off the high hills bordering Lake Rosseau.

In complete contrast to the fury of Rosseau, two delightful little waterfalls on the nearby Skeleton River have won hundreds of fans for their quiet enchantment. Both the Hatchery Falls and Minnehaha Falls cascade through sun-dappled shadows of overhanging birch, maple and hemlock. Like High Falls on the Oxtongue, these falls invite quiet contemplation and stir more subtle emotions.

West of Lake Muskoka along the big outlet rivers, the Moon and Musquash, almost a dozen waterfalls and rapids provide a dramatic display of some of Nature's most powerful elements: huge quantities of water, masses of ancient rock and towering wind-swept pines. These elements are all present along the three channels of Bala Falls right at the outlet of Lake Muskoka; here, however, the scenery has been greatly altered by dams, bridges and urban development over the last 120 years. The fourth largest in the Muskoka watershed, Bala Falls bears some historical resemblance to Bracebridge Falls. It too sparked the initial growth of the town around it and was harnessed to run a pioneer sawmill

ROSSEAU FALLS, *Rosseau River. In the spring this normally docile falls explodes into an awesome series of untamed chutes.*

THE HATCHERY FALLS, *Skeleton River. The pristine beauty of this enchanting cascade speaks for itself.*

as well as hydroelectric stations that generated the first electricity for the local residents.

Below the forks where the Musquash branches off, the Moon carries large quantities of water only in the spring, due to the Ontario Hydro diversion. But during that season few waterfalls can match 12-metre-high (39-foot) Moon Falls near the mouth of the river. In an awesome display of raw power the water blasts out between bald rock slopes dotted with ground-hugging junipers and weather-beaten pine — a starkly beautiful panorama so characteristic of the Georgian Bay shore regions and so different from anything else in the watershed. Few people get the opportunity to view this remote natural wonder at the height of its springtime magnificence.

Not far away, on the Musquash River, another powerful and very striking waterfall, Sandy Gray's Chute, usually carries abundant water all year. Plunging just 5.5 metres (18 feet) it nonetheless roars with a vengeance through a narrow gap between the rocky, pine-fringed shores of Gray Lake above and Flatrock Lake below. The chute is every bit as wild today as it was in 1867, when log-driver Sandy Gray lost his life there in an ill-fated attempt to break a logjam. Early campers claimed that Sandy Gray's ghost subsequently haunted this rugged section of the Musquash River.

It would take an entire book to adequately describe all the fine waterfalls the Muskoka River offers for scenic viewing. I've touched only the highlights of one of Muskoka's most valuable resources. Many smaller falls and chutes have delighted sightseers over the years and contributed to the economy by providing power for pioneer mills. Let these be an unexpected bonus when you discover them in the course of a hike, a paddle or a drive through any part of Muskoka.

MOON FALLS (LOWER CHUTE), *Moon River. Sloping expanses of bald rock and huge quantities of spring meltwaters create a compelling scene that speaks eloquently of the wild, rugged beauty of the Georgian Bay shore regions.*

MUSKOKA RIVER WATERFALLS

The twelve largest plus selected other waterfalls. Size (power) at average stream flow. (D) — hydroelectric dam makes up much or all of the descent.

Waterfall	River	Size (power) kilowatts	Height metres	feet
South Falls	S. Muskoka	8,900	33.2	109
Ragged Rapids (D)	Musquash	6,200	11.3	37
Big Eddy (D)	Musquash	6,100	11.0	36
Bala Falls	Moon	4,400	6.0	20
Bracebridge Falls	N. Muskoka	4,200	16.0	52
High Falls	N. Muskoka	3,700	14.6	48
Matthias Falls (D)	S. Muskoka	3,500	13.4	44
Wilson's Falls	N. Muskoka	3,300	12.5	41
Sandy Gray's Chute	Musquash	3,100	5.5	18
Trethewey Falls (D)	S. Muskoka	2,800	10.7	35
Hanna Chute (D)	S. Muskoka	2,600	9.8	32
Moon Falls	Moon	2,500	12.0	39
Ragged Falls	Oxtongue	1,900	25.0	82
Distress Chutes	Big East	1,300	18.0	59
High Falls	Oxtongue	740	10.0	33
Hogs' Trough	Oxtongue	740	8.0	26
Long Slide Chute	Hollow	500	8.0	26
Rosseau Falls	Rosseau	390	19.0	62
Hatchery Falls	Skeleton	90	7.0	23

ORIGINAL BIRD WOOLLEN MILL in the 1870s. One of the most attractive water mills in Muskoka, this pine-framed building stood just below the road bridge at the top of Bracebridge Falls. The headrace that conveyed water to it still exists.

· Archives of Ontario Acc. 15963-23

CHAPTER 8

From Waterwheel to Turbine: The Water Mill Era on the Muskoka River

Man first began to harness the energy of rivers at least two thousand years ago. By the second century B.C. civilizations in the great river valleys of the Middle East were using waterwheels propelled by river currents to lift water for irrigation. By the first century B.C. water power was being utilized to turn millstones to grind grain into flour. The first water-powered grist mills probably originated in the mountainous regions to the north and west of India, but they quickly spread throughout Europe and Asia. Small and simple, suited for use on steep, fast-flowing creeks, these mills employed a horizontal waterwheel connected directly to the millstones above by a vertical axle.

Also in the first century B.C. the Romans made an important technological advance when they adapted the more versatile vertical waterwheel to turn the millstones by means of shafts and speed-increasing gears. That basic technology would remain virtually unchanged, grinding most of the grain in developed regions, right up until little more than a hundred years ago.

From Roman times to the 19th century water power remained the prime mover of world industry. Initially used just to grind grain and raise water for irrigation, the waterwheel increasingly served to drive machinery for a wide range of industrial processes that included smelting iron, shaping iron implements, crushing everything from rocks to olives, sawing lumber, fulling cloth and, by the early 1800s, powering a variety of processes in cotton and woollen mills.

The French colonists established the first water-powered mills in Canada in the early 1600s, sawmills and grist mills to serve the new settlements in Quebec and the Maritimes. Not until the 1780s, when the United Empire Loyalists moved north into Canada, were the first water mills built in what is now Ontario. By the mid-1850s Ontario boasted 1,449 water-powered sawmills, 610 grist mills (most water-powered) and smaller numbers of other types of water mills.

During the 1800s the steam engine overtook and surpassed the energy of falling water as the most important source of industrial power — just one consequence of the Industrial Revolution. Water-power technology itself underwent major changes during that period, the most far-reaching being the introduction of the hydraulic turbine. Compact and powerful, reliable and efficient, the turbine rapidly supplanted the traditional waterwheel after 1850 and gave the water-powered mills a new but relatively short-lived lease on life.

At the time the settlement of Muskoka began, in 1859, water power was still highly regarded in Ontario despite the increasing use of steam power in many places. The province boasted numerous fast-flowing streams and waterfalls and it made sense to use this free source of energy whenever possible. This was particularly the case in a frontier area like Muskoka, where poor transportation facilities made it difficult to bring in heavy steam-powered machinery and where initially only small quantities of power were required anyway. Water-wheels, shafts and gearing could be fashioned largely of wood from the surrounding forests, with only such items as saw blades and millstones having to be hauled in. Water power was a simple, proven technology ideally suited to the small pioneer mill.

Enterprising Muskoka settlers quickly took advantage of the numerous waterfalls and rapids on the Muskoka River and its tributaries. Small sawmills sprang up to cut lumber for frontier farms and hamlets. Grist mills were erected soon afterwards to grind wheat and other grains from new fields hacked out of the wilderness. Such mills obviously made life much easier for the pioneers during the harsh early years of settlement in the district.

Several of the early Muskoka River water mills became the starting points for new communities. Bracebridge, Port Sydney, Baysville, Bala, Hoodstown, Matthiasville and Dee Bank all began to grow around the nucleus of one or more water mills, though after promising beginnings the latter three never really amounted to much.

Altogether at least 29 water mills were built in the Muskoka River system. The majority were sawmills or combined sawmills and grist mills. Grist mills and one woollen mill made up the rest. Most were just small country mills catering to the nearby farmers and crossroads hamlets. A couple of them, however, did grow into quite substantial operations, marketing their products beyond Muskoka District.

Water-powered industry reached a brief zenith on the Muskoka River during the 1870s and 1880s, then declined without ever reaching its full potential. The watershed was too remote and sparsely populated to support the diversity and number of industries found further south, the waterfalls themselves frequently hard to reach or surrounded by rocky precipitous terrain ill-suited to the construction of mills or factories. More significantly, the arrival of the railway (1875) and the expansion of steamboat navigation on the lakes made it feasible to establish large steam-powered mills and factories in Muskoka. With the dawn of the 20th century, electric motors and internal combustion engines also began to play an increasing industrial role in Muskoka and throughout the industrialized world.

By the early 1920s only about seven water mills remained on the Muskoka River. The last of these finally closed their doors in 1954. The water-mill era on the river had lasted just a century. A few commercial water mills still operate in Canada today, and many more in some less industrialized countries, but water power now is used primarily to generate electricity.

When we think of the old water mills we often harbour romantic images of stately stone buildings by the river's edge, big wooden waterwheels turning ponderously in the mill race, shady willows overhanging a quiet mill pond. There were mills like that — but not on the Muskoka River. The typical Muskoka mill was a wooden barn-like structure, strictly functional in design, surrounded, in the case of sawmills, by acres of log dumps, lumber piles and slabs. Although some of the earliest mills used the age-old waterwheel (usually one of the overshot design), the majority were equipped with or converted to the superior, but rather less romantic, hydraulic turbine.

The technology employed in some of the first frontier water mills on the Muskoka River was actually quite primitive. Many of the early sawmills, besides using waterwheels, were equipped with the old "mulley" or upright saw. In this system, a single saw blade mounted in a wooden frame jerked up and down, slowly cutting a plank as the log inched forward on the carriage. A rod and crank drove the saw, a ratchet mechanism the carriage, both connected to the waterwheel. This technology was only a little more advanced than that found in the first water-powered sawmills of 15th-century Europe, but it worked and most of the parts could be fashioned on-site out of wood.

These simple little mills, usually just one- or two-man operations, could only cut 1,000 to 2,000 feet of lumber per day. Still, they were a vast improvement on hand-sawing and perfectly suited to a fledgling pioneer economy. Later many of these mills were expanded and larger ones built which used turbines to spin large circular saws (waterwheels were also used to run circular saws, but production was less). Even these bigger mills, however, were very modest operations compared with the large steam-powered sawmills that became prevalent in Muskoka after 1875. Only one water-powered sawmill on the Muskoka River matched the scale of those steam-driven establishments.

There has always been a place in the Muskoka economy for the small country sawmill, and a few exist today, similar in size and appearance to the water-powered variety except that they use a gas or diesel engine instead of a turbine. The water-powered sawmill disappeared not because the water-power technology became outmoded, but due to the death or retirement of owners, lack of business, or destruction of the mill by fire or flooding. Today it is simply more convenient to rely on a motor rather than on a hydraulic turbine. Anyone contemplating a water-powered sawmill now would

in any case face a tangle of bureaucratic red tape before the project even got started.

Water-powered grist mills on the Muskoka River, and elsewhere, also disappeared due to factors unrelated to water-power technology. In Muskoka such mills enjoyed modest success for two or three decades after settlement began. Pioneer farmers grew respectable quantities of wheat, corn, barley, rye and oats, and the local country grist mills, producing both flour and livestock feed, were a vital part of the economy.

By the 1880s, however, the district was readily accessible by rail, and pure white flour could be obtained from merchants. For the most part, the local mills could not produce this highly refined product for which consumers had developed an enormous preference. To compound the situation, grain production in Muskoka declined as the century wore on. Lack of business ultimately forced several Muskoka River grist mills to close by the 1890s. Those operated in conjunction with sawmills survived longer, sometimes until the sawmills closed. Most of them ended their days chopping livestock feed.

All of the Muskoka River grist mills (indeed most grist mills everywhere until the late 19th century) used stone-milling technology not much different from that developed by the Romans 2,000 years before. Certainly the grinding process itself, known as low-milling, was virtually unchanged. The grain, fed into a hole in the centre of an upper rotating millstone, was ground between that upper stone and a lower stationary one as it passed out to the circumference. The resulting flour was then bolted and sifted to remove the coarse bran. In the larger commercial mills a variety of automated conveyors, lifts and gravity-feed chutes

SAWMILL AT PORT SYDNEY FALLS, *c. 1872. Pioneer settler John McAlpine built this mill in 1868-69. In appearance and construction it is fairly typical of Muskoka River water-powered sawmills. A turbine drives the circular saw.*

- George H. Johnson

moved grain and flour through the mill. Such technology had been developed in the United States in the late 1700s and was probably employed in the big grist mills at Bracebridge, Port Sydney and Dee Bank. In the smaller operations the miller relied largely on his muscles. Muskoka River millers used both waterwheels and turbines to turn the heavy millstones, which typically measured 1.2 metres (4 feet) in diameter and rotated 125 to 150 revolutions per minute. The small mills had just one set, or "run," of stones, the larger ones had two or more. The stones were usually imported from Europe.

The stone-ground low-milling process could not produce the pure white flour demanded by consumers, nor was it ideally suited to the hard wheats being grown in North America. By the last quarter of the 19th century, however, a new flour-making process had been perfected which overcame these problems. This was the roller mill, in which the grain moved through sets of iron rollers and then into elaborate sifting and purifying equipment.

Roller mills needed to operate on a much larger scale than the little country grist mills such as those on the Muskoka River did, and required a considerable capital investment. In Muskoka, only the big grist mill at Bracebridge made the conversion, still retaining water power, however. As supplies of Muskoka wheat dwindled in the 1890s it had to rely on wheat brought in by rail from western Canada.

The most famous water mill on the Muskoka River was neither a sawmill nor a grist mill, but a woollen mill. Water power had been used for centuries for at least one process in the woollen industry — fulling mills operated in Italy by the 10th century. Later, as the Industrial Revolution began, machines were perfected for other processes in the production of cloth, initially for the cotton industry, then adapted for woollen production. In the 1800s large woollen mills combining all the various processes under one roof became common. In Canada this factory system didn't become prevalent until the last half of the century, although mills carrying out individual processes were built earlier to complement what was largely a home industry initially. Woollen mills used steam power or water power, the latter more common in the smaller establishments that sprang up in numerous communities across southern Ontario.

Details of the growth and decline of the Muskoka River's only woollen mill are included in the following section, which gives a brief history of all the water mills known to have operated on the river.

THE MUSKOKA RIVER WATER MILLS

Practically all of the Muskoka River water mills were built in the 1860s and 1870s, the first two decades of settlement on the Muskoka frontier. The very first water mill, however, preceded settlement by six years and was a result of lumbering expansion.

In the early 1850s a Penetanguishene entrepreneur and local politician named William Hamilton began to eye the virgin pine growing along the lower reaches of the Musquash River near Georgian Bay. Lumbermen had not yet touched the huge reserves of pine in the Muskoka watershed; this valuable resource must have beckoned enticingly from Penetanguishene, just 23 kilometres (14 miles) across an arm of Georgian Bay. In late 1853 Hamilton took the first step towards exploiting it. He built a small water-powered sawmill at Three Rock Chute about three kilometres (2 miles)

GRIST-MILL STONES *from the Gammage mill, Baysville. Millstones quite commonly were made of carefully fitted chunks of stone rather than from a single block. This usually indicates the use of a special quartz, found in France, which millers considered superior to other kinds of rock. The centre pieces of the Gammage stones are missing. Although not evident, these 1.2-metre-diameter (4-foot) stones would be about .3 metres (1 foot) thick. Note the radiating pattern of grooves, the dressing - which facilitated the grinding process.*

MUSKOKA MILLS. *This sketch, made from an old photograph, shows the huge water-powered sawmill that once operated at the mouth of the Musquash River. Details in the photograph suggest this is the downstream side of the mill. Whirling saws inside ripped Muskoka pine into more than 50,000 board feet of lumber every working day.*

upstream from Georgian Bay and soon began cutting pine nearby. Lumber from the mill was rafted down the river to Georgian Bay.

The Three Rock Chute mill, built on an island at the falls, was the first manufacturing establishment of any sort in the Muskoka watershed. It operated only a few years. However, not far downstream from Three Rock Chute, at the mouth of the Musquash, a vastly larger water-powered sawmill was built in the late 1850s (or possibly in the early 1860s). This operation and the sizable settlement that grew up around it was known as Muskoka Mills.

Like Hamilton's mill, the Muskoka Mills resulted entirely from lumbering expansion, not frontier settlement. Big lumber companies had begun major logging operations in the Muskoka watershed in the 1850s, and since the river provided the only feasible way of getting the logs out in those early years, the river mouth was a logical place for a mill. From this spot lumber could be easily shipped across Georgian Bay by boat. The lack of a natural falls here was evidently solved by building a dam (minor rapids downstream from Three Rock Chute don't have enough drop by themselves).

The Muskoka Mills was by far the largest water-powered sawmill ever to operate in the Muskoka watershed. At the time of the 1871 Census of Canada it employed a work force of 82 and in a six-month operating season produced 8,500,000 feet of lumber from 80,000 pine logs. The mill's water turbines developed a total of 250 horsepower. The big lumber firm of Hotchkiss, Hughson and Company operated the facility in 1871; however, the original owner was apparently the Muskoka Milling and Lumber Company.

Although initially ideal for processing Muskoka pine, the location of the Muskoka Mills later became a liability. Depletion of the pine in the western part of the watershed forced the lumber companies to move logging operations further east; that meant longer, more difficult and expensive log drives down to Georgian Bay. When the railway was extended into the heart of the Muskoka watershed — to Lake Muskoka at Gravenhurst — in 1875, it made more sense to establish big mills there, thus eliminating the need to float logs another 36 kilometres (22 miles) down the Musquash.

Before the end of the 19th century, quantities of pine sufficient to feed the Muskoka Mills could no longer be economically obtained from the Muskoka watershed, and the operation closed down. Strung out along the barren, rocky shores of Georgian Bay, the once bustling mill community quickly became a ghost town.

Comparatively little pioneer settlement took place on the rocky, infertile lands between Lake Muskoka and Georgian Bay. The only other mill to harness the powerful waterfalls of the Moon and Musquash rivers was one at Bala Falls, right at the outlet of Lake Muskoka. That was the Thomas Burgess sawmill.

Burgess, a Scot, first came to Lake Muskoka in 1868, the year the Ontario government instigated the main movement of settlers to Muskoka by passing the Free Grant and Homesteads Act. Impressed by the beauty, water power and strategic location of the falls at the outlet of the lake, Burgess soon moved his family upcountry and by 1870 was operating a sawmill on the small northern channel of the falls (known ever since as the Millstream). He also established a store. By these events, the community of Bala was born (it's named after Bala Lake in Wales). The Burgess family would remain in the forefront of Bala affairs for several decades. Thomas died in 1901, six years before the arrival of the Canadian Pacific Railway really sparked the growth of the little hamlet.

Most settlement in the Muskoka River watershed took place between the Muskoka Lakes and the rugged country rising to the east of Lake of Bays. That's where settlers built the rest of the water mills. Numerous waterfalls on the North and South Muskoka and their tributaries became mill sites; so too did falls on the tributaries of the Indian River, specifically on the Dee and Shadow rivers.

Despite its modest size, the Dee River system supported five water mills. The land in that part of Muskoka, around Three Mile Lake in Watt Township, ranked among the best for farming in the district. It filled up quickly. Indeed, settlers began moving into the Dee basin in the early 1860s, several years before the area was officially opened for settlement. Jacob Bogart arrived first in 1862. It was either Bogart or another Watt Township pioneer, Thomas Yates, or possibly the two of them in partnership, who established a water-powered sawmill at a cascade on Camel Creek (a tiny stream that tumbles from Camel Lake down into Three Mile). One source indicates this mill was built in the mid-1860s, a primitive little operation equipped with waterwheel and upright saw; however, it is not listed in the 1871 Census of Canada (which provides details of the various mills in the district) and may not have been established until the 1870s.

In any event, Bogart acquired full ownership of the mill in 1877 and the operation continued until 1924, one of Bogart's sons running it in the later years. At the time it closed, the mill occupied quite a large wooden building and had a 60-horsepower turbine and circular saw. The old dam and mill pond at the top of the cascade, the massive stone foundations of the mill itself, as well as the remains of the penstock and turbine, can still be seen immediately south of the Windermere Road where it crosses Camel Creek. These are the most extensive ruins of any of the water mills that operated in the Muskoka River watershed.

Another early settler in Watt Township was Archie Taylor. By 1870 — possibly as early as 1865 — he had built a small sawmill at the waterfall at the mouth of the Dee River on Lake Rosseau. One of the smallest of the 11 water mills operating in the Muskoka watershed at the time of the 1871 Census, it later grew into a much larger operation, a turbine and circular saw replacing the original waterwheel and mulley.

Although it was established by Taylor, this long-time fixture at the mouth of the Dee became better known as the Clark mill. Thomas Clark purchased it in 1885, and the Clark family — Thomas and later his son Thomas Henry Clark — ran it for the next 44 years, until it burned down in 1929. Some of the mill foundations can still be seen at the foot of the falls (known as Clark Falls) on the north side. A stone dam at the top, built around 1918 to replace an older timber structure, still holds back the waters of Clark Pond above. Concrete saddles that supported the penstock leading down to the mill turbine remain in place on the rock beside the falls.

One of the most interesting chapters in the history of the Dee River unfolded around the other major waterfall on the pastoral stream, Dee Bank Falls at the outlet of Three Mile Lake. In 1868 or shortly afterwards a newcomer to the area, John Shannon, harnessed the south channel of this picturesque set of rapids and chutes to run a busy sawmill (in 1871 it employed ''five men and one boy''). That, however, was only the beginning. Encouraged by the number of farmers settling in the Three Mile Lake area and the amount of grain

THE SHANNON MILLS at Dee Bank Village, 1870s. The big grist mill built by John Shannon stands 3½ storeys high in the centre of this Seymour Penson drawing, at the foot of Dee Bank Falls. To the left of it you can see Shannon's sawmill (but not the south channel of the falls, on which it was located). You can also see the wooden flume that carried water from a dam at the sawmill to the grist-mill turbine. Part of the bridge across the top of the falls is visible in the lower left. Little evidence of once thriving Dee Bank remains amid the woods and grassy slopes around the falls today.
- from the *Guide Book and Atlas of Muskoka and Parry Sound Districts*, 1879

being grown, Shannon embarked on a much more ambitious project: a big water-powered grist mill at the foot of the falls.

It must have been a proud moment for John Shannon in 1871 when the millstones rumbled into action for the first time. The new mill was a handsome timber-framed structure, three-and-one-half storeys high and reputed to be one of the largest and most modern in the north country at that time. It was only the second grist mill in all of Muskoka.

Around the Shannon mills the village of Dee Bank grew. A thriving little settlement by the late 1870s, it seemed destined to become a centre of some importance. Twenty years later it was practically a ghost town. In the 1880s nearby Windermere on Lake Rosseau began to rise to prominence

around the nucleus of a major resort (Windermere House). From its inland location Dee Bank village could not tap into the growing tourism trade. As its forestry and grain-growing base in the Dee basin declined, so too did the community. By the early 1890s the stones in the grist mill lay still and silent.

Possibly the last water mill built in the Muskoka watershed was erected in the Dee River basin in 1896 — ironically, by one of the earliest settlers in Muskoka. John Lillie Shea arrived in Watt Township with his parents and brothers in 1863. Thirty-three years later he built a water-powered sawmill at Sherwood's Falls on Sherwood's Creek, a southern tributary to Three Mile Lake. The mill operated for only a few years.

For a number of years another water-powered sawmill worked busily at a falls on the Shadow River, the little stream flowing into the north end of Lake Rosseau. Ebenezer Sirett built this mill, probably in the latter half of the 1860s, a few kilometres above Lake Rosseau in Humphrey Township. Sirett was one of the first settlers in that area. Arriving in 1864, he soon took up several lots made available along the Parry Sound Road, then being built from Muskoka to Parry Sound village. According to the 1871 Census the mill employed four men and cut 200,000 feet of lumber per season. Sirett and his wife are among those interred in a small cemetery not far from the old mill site.

Turning our attention to the South Muskoka River system, we find that at least six water mills operated in that part of the Muskoka watershed. Four of these harnessed waterfalls on the South Muskoka mainstream below Lake of Bays. The earliest was a tiny sawmill erected at Trethewey Falls around 1865 by James Trethewey. The Tretheweys could count themselves among the earliest settlers along the South Muskoka in Draper Township. They farmed land near the falls and of course James ran his mill, which by 1871 was still basically a one-man operation sawing lumber for nearby settlers. In the 1880s Trethewey moved to British Columbia, but other owners continued the operation for at least another decade. The mill site, on the northern channel of the falls, is now occupied by a hydroelectric station.

At the next waterfall upstream from Trethewey, Matthias Falls, another Draper Township pioneer had a little sawmill in operation by 1870, similar in size to James Trethewey's mill. During the 1870s, however, William Matthias considerably expanded his operation and incorporated a grist mill into it as well. Matthias comes across in the records as a versatile man: preacher, carpenter, blacksmith, miller, storekeeper. He built a church, store and blacksmith shop near the rough little chute that powered his mills and in 1880 filed subdivision plans for Matthiasville.

Matthiasville never really became anything more than a small hamlet. Uffington, just to the south, was the principal settlement in the area. The Matthiasville mills, however, remained a going concern. Statistics compiled in 1897 indicate the sawmill employed 12 men and could produce 10,000 feet of lumber per day. In the early 1900s William Matthias' son Samuel ran the mills as a woodworking and feed-chopping business. As at Trethewey Falls, the old mill site, on the west bank of the chute, is now occupied by a hydroelectric station.

Although Matthiasville never achieved great importance, another village on the South Muskoka that grew around water mills fared better: Baysville at the outlet of Lake of Bays. In 1870 a low waterfall there attracted the interest of William Brown, a sawyer from near Brantford, Ontario. Deciding that the site would be a good one for a mill and village, he obtained the adjacent Free Grant lots, moved his family up in 1872, and built a dam and sawmill. The arrival of the mill machinery in 1873 over a newly cut road from Bracebridge put him in business.

That same year, 1873, Brown first filed subdivision plans for Baysville. The village grew and thrived around Brown's sawmill and a water-powered grist mill built in 1877 by William Gammage. Brown's mill sat at the west end of the dam (remnants of its foundation can still be seen in the bedrock below the present Baysville Dam). The grist mill sat at the east end; no trace of it remains there, but its millstones are

MATTHIASVILLE *in the 1870s. A turbulent little chute on the South Muskoka River here powered William Matthias' sawmill and grist mill (the large wooden building beside the river just to the right of centre in the picture). A dike beside the river impounded a mill pond (lower left). Water probably entered the pond from the river at the top of the falls, by the bridge, then discharged through the mill turbine. A big hydroelectric dam and powerhouse now dominates this scene.*

· Drawing by Seymour Penson in the *Guide Book and Atlas of Muskoka and Parry Sound Districts, 1879*

BROWN'S SAWMILL AND DAM, Baysville. William Brown, founder of Baysville, built the first dam here in 1872 and had his mill operating the year after. The dam raised the water level enough to run the mill turbine; only a very low waterfall existed naturally.

· Archives of Ontario Acc. 2839-28

SAWMILL AT BAYSVILLE DAM. Closed for several years and falling apart at the time of the photograph (1948), this mill was a descendant of the original water-powered operation established by William Brown in 1873. The stone dam, built in 1918 by the Department of Public Works, replaced Brown's old timber dam.

· Ontario Hydro

incorporated into a monument near the Highway 117 bridge just upstream. The sawmill operated much longer than the grist mill, continuing for a number of years after William Brown retired and sold it in 1914. Baysville's strategic location at the foot of Lake of Bays allowed it to survive the closing of the mills by catering to the growing resort and tourism trade.

Because settlement never penetrated very far east of Lake of Bays, the considerable water-power potential of its two main tributaries, the Oxtongue and Hollow rivers, went largely untapped. But on the fringes of settlement near their mouths, each did support one water-powered mill.

Around 1877 George F. Marsh built a sawmill at the first falls (Marsh's Falls) above Lake of Bays on the Oxtongue, just south of Dwight. Marsh is probably best known for his leading role in the steamship navigation business on Lake of Bays and over Peninsula and Fairy lakes to Huntsville, and for spearheading the construction of the Portage Railway between Lake of Bays and Peninsula Lake. These activities occupied him from 1884 until his death in 1904. One of his sons operated the sawmill into the 1890s. The mill stood on the north shore of the Marsh's Falls plunge pool. Marsh's first steamboat, the *Mary Louise*, was launched there in 1884.

The only water mill to operate on the Hollow River was James B. Shrigley's combined sawmill and grist mill. Built in 1874, it was the first mill in the Dorset area. It stood not far upstream from the mouth of the Hollow River about two kilometres (1.2 miles) east of Dorset. Shrigley didn't harness a natural waterfalls. He simply put a dam across the river at the site of a minor riffle to raise the necessary head of water for the waterwheel or turbine. Faint traces of the dam can still be found there.

Of the nearly 30 water-powered mills established in the Muskoka River watershed, half were on the North Muskoka and its tributaries. These included some of the largest and most famous water mills in Muskoka District.

Without doubt Bracebridge Falls near the mouth of the North Muskoka became the most prominent water-milling centre in the district. A sawmill and grist mill there, the first in the newly opened townships of Muskoka, provided the initial impetus for the settlement that would become the thriving town of Bracebridge, and a water-powered woollen mill grew into one of the town's leading industries.

The beginnings of a settlement were evident by 1862 beside the powerful and strategically located North Falls (as Bracebridge Falls was known before 1864). That year Alexander Bailey, operator of a fur-trading post further down-river, began building a water-powered sawmill at the foot of the falls. Soon the upright saw in this little frontier mill was cutting 1,000 feet of lumber per day for the fledgling settlement.

Bailey is credited with building the first grist mill at Bracebridge Falls as well. It ground its first bushels of grain in 1865. Until the Shannon grist mill at Dee Bank opened in 1871, the Bracebridge Falls mill was the only grist mill in Muskoka. The 2,000 bushels of wheat, rye, oats, peas and corn brought to it in 1870 gives a rough indication of the modest amount of grain being grown in the district at that early date.

When the 1871 Census was taken, both sawmill and grist mill were owned by Thomas Myers and Robert E. Perry, who had purchased them two years earlier. By then the sawmill had expanded into a 250,000-foot-per-year operation and production of 1,000,000 feet of lumber was expected for the

GRIST MILL AT BRACEBRIDGE FALLS. In this 1890s view of the falls you can see the tall wooden grist-mill building rising from the water's edge at the bottom. A water-powered sawmill formerly stood immediately to the right of it. Note the log slide on the opposite side of the falls.

· Ken Veitch/Town of Bracebridge

next season. Both mills sat at the bottom of the falls on the east side. The larger grist mill was a gaunt 3½-storey wooden structure that towered over the waterfront.

Although the sawmill operation was discontinued within a few years, the grist mill grew and thrived for nearly four more decades. From humble beginnings as a country mill employing the age-old stone-milling process, it eventually grew into a modern operation using the new roller-mill technology. The conversion from stones to iron rollers occurred by 1890 or so. In the early 1900s, operating with five sets of double rollers, the Bracebridge Flour Mill was producing 100 barrels of flour per day. By that time most of the wheat was imported by rail from western Canada.

It's hard to say how long the flour mill might have operated had a spectacular fire not destroyed it in 1909. The owner decided not to rebuild due to the difficulty of competing with the large steam-powered flour mills in the cities.

The most famous water mill at Bracebridge Falls, indeed in all of Muskoka, was the Bird Woollen Mill. When Henry J. Bird came to Bracebridge in 1872 to establish this mill, he probably had no inkling his modest water-powered operation would grow into one of Muskoka's leading manufacturing establishments with a market and reputation all across Canada. By all accounts a determined, industrious and innovative man, Bird himself would become one of the leading citizens of Bracebridge.

A native of Woodchester, England, where he learned the woollen mill trade in his father's mills, Bird briefly owned a woollen mill at Glen Allan, Ontario, before relocating to Bracebridge. He was attracted by the water-power potential of the falls and the sheep-raising potential of Muskoka. He built his new mill near the top of the falls on the west bank.

It was a sturdy wooden structure of a simple but pleasing design, measuring 9 by 15 metres, or 30 by 50 feet (fairly typical dimensions for Muskoka River mills), and standing 3½ storeys high. The building served not only as a place of business but for ten years as Bird's residence too. In 1882 Bird moved his family into his new Woodchester Villa high atop the hill overlooking the mill. Now restored, this unique octagonal house is operated as a museum by the Bracebridge Historical Society.

In the early years the Bird Woollen Mill operated on a relatively small-scale custom basis, carding raw wool for local farmers, later producing mill-spun yard and eventually weaving cloth. The various processes involved were carried out on machines powered by the mill turbine through an arrangement of shafts, gears and belts. To insure a supply of wool, Bird helped many Muskoka farmers establish flocks of sheep.

As time went by, Bird expanded production to include a wide range of tweeds, flannels, blankets and cloth for the famous mackinaw coats so popular with the lumbermen. His durable high-quality goods found a market throughout Canada. By the First World War the mill had grown into a sprawling factory beside the falls, the newer stone, brick and concrete additions virtually surrounding the original wooden building. It employed as many as 60 men and women. During the war the mill supplied blankets to Canadian, British and French troops. Business remained brisk in the 1920s, although a decline in Muskoka sheep farming meant that increasing quantities of wool had to be imported.

The Depression brought hard times from which the Bird Woollen Mill never fully recovered. Bird himself died in 1936, leaving the operation of the mill to his sons. In the coming years several factors combined to slowly bring about

BIRD WOOLLEN MILL, *final version. By 1912 extensive masonry additions had transformed the mill into this large factory, photographed here from the railway bridge over Bracebridge Falls. The roof of the original 1872 mill pokes above the sprawling expansions.* · Archives of Ontario Acc. 15963-13

BIRD WOOLLEN MILL INTERIOR, 1914. The man standing on the right is Henry Bird. Note the complex arrangement of belts and shafts that transmitted power from the mill turbine to the various machines.

· Archives of Ontario Acc. 15963-19

the demise of the once thriving business. The federal government removed tariffs that had protected the Canadian textile industry, and the introduction of synthetic fabrics further increased competition. A lack of government contracts in the Second World War didn't help the mill's finances either. In the mill itself antiquated equipment and the retirement of the older skilled workers caused production quality to decline. Finally, in 1954, 82 years after it opened, the Bird Woollen Mill closed forever. In 1967 the town of Bracebridge razed the deteriorating main mill complex and subsequently turned the site into a parking lot. All that remains is a concrete storage building on the opposite side of the railway tracks, used now as a warehouse.

In addition to the saw, grist and woollen mills at Bracebridge Falls, one other water mill operated within Bracebridge. For a brief period in the mid-1870s the firm of Halstead and McNicol ran a mill beside a dam at Halstead's Rapids, about a kilometre upstream from Bracebridge Falls. Details about this mill are sketchy. It may have been a sawmill or, according to one source, a furniture factory.

Still quite close to Bracebridge on the North Muskoka, the splendid cataract known as Wilson's Falls supported a water mill for at least 30 years. Sometime in the latter 1860s two Bracebridge men, Gilman Wilson and his son-in-law William Holditch, established the Norwood Mills on a small secondary channel of the falls. A substantial saw, shingle and siding mill, it was first powered by a large overshot waterwheel, then re-equipped with a turbine during reconstruction after an 1870 fire. Census data for 1871 shows the mill employed four men and produced 240,000 feet of lumber and 600 bundles of lath in a year — a large operation by Muskoka standards of that day. The mill sat just behind the present hydroelectric station at Wilson's Falls.

The sawmill business was quite a change for Gilman Wilson, who had first come to Muskoka in 1862 as a Methodist Episcopal minister. He retired from active ministry work in 1865 for health reasons. Holditch, who married Wilson's daughter Elizabeth in 1866, was an ambitious young man who involved himself in a wide variety of ventures in Bracebridge after arriving there in the early 1860s.

In the 1870s Holditch, then Wilson, gave up their interests in the Norwood Mills. Other operators continued to run it afterwards. In the 1890s Hamlet Wolfram was running it as a shingle mill. He rebuilt it after another fire in 1892.

Much further up the North Muskoka River, a waterfalls at the outlet of Mary Lake spawned an important water mill complex around which the village of Port Sydney grew. In 1868 pioneer settler John McAlpine trekked into this scenic location and began building a sawmill on the small island separating the two channels of the chute. Equipped with a 40-horsepower turbine and circular saw, the mill cut its first plank in December 1869 and was soon busily producing lumber at a rate of 250,000 feet per year.

Growth and prosperity, however, didn't come until after Albert Sydney-Smith arrived in 1871 and took over the mill. Young, ambitious and financially well-off, Sydney-Smith envisioned a village springing up around his business (settlement at that time was concentrating just to the north on Mary Lake). Accordingly, in 1873 he subdivided some of the land around the falls for the village of Port Sydney (it was subsequently amalgamated with the adjacent Mary Lake settlement under the single name of Port sydney).

At about the same time, Sydney-Smith began a major

SYDNEY-SMITH'S MILLS, *Port Sydney Falls, c. 1900. This large complex housed a sawmill (on the right, with the jackladder to carry logs in) and a grist mill-oatmeal mill (in the left half of the structure). Present-day Port Sydney Falls spills down behind the mills; a second channel of the falls, on the near side of the mills, is blocked off now.*

· George H. Johnson

expansion of his mill. By 1876 the original sawmill had grown into an imposing industrial complex at the falls, housing a revamped sawmill, grist mill and oatmeal mill (the latter just a specialized grist mill). This nucleus helped make Port Sydney one of the more important settlements in Muskoka for a few years.

With a capacity of 10,000 feet of lumber per day, the Sydney-Smith sawmill was one of the larger water-powered sawmills in the Muskoka watershed. The grist mill was also a substantial operation in its heyday, producing Staff of Life brand flour from local and imported western wheat. In later years it was reduced to chopping animal feed. Sydney-Smith's mill complex required two turbines of 175-horsepower total capacity to run all the machinery.

The death of Albert Sydney-Smith in 1925 essentially spelled the end for his mills; they were torn down in 1930. An attractive little park now occupies the old mill site beside the falls. Port Sydney village lives on as a thriving residential and resort community nestled at the foot of beautiful Mary Lake.

In 1873, as Albert Sydney-Smith was making plans for his new mills, members of the pioneer Fetterley family were busy building a dam and water-powered sawmill at some rapids on the North Muskoka River above Mary Lake, just south of Huntsville (which at that time was just an insignificant little hamlet). A year or two later they added stones for grinding grain, as no other grist mills yet existed in northern Muskoka. Between 1873 and 1875 a government navigation lock and short canal were constructed to by-pass the rapids at the Fetterleys' mill (not surprisingly the mill later became known as the Locks Mill).

John L. Fetterley ran the Locks Mill until the 1880s, then it had a succession of owners before Benjamin Cottrill acquired it in 1907. The Cottrill family operated it for nearly half a century. Under their ownership the Locks Mill grew into a sawmilling operation that rivalled the size of Port Sydney and Matthiasville sawmills in their heyday. The mill building itself sat at the east end of the control dam on the river side of the canal leading to the lock.

The useful life of the Locks Mill, the longest surviving water-powered sawmill on the Muskoka River, essentially came to an end in 1954, when part of the foundations collapsed. In 1955 the Department of Public Works tore it down and began rehabilitating the mill yards to create an attractive park around the lock site.

Early settlers across northern Muskoka in Sinclair, Chaffey and Stisted townships were served by several small sawmills and grist mills built at waterfalls on streams feeding into the North Muskoka River system. One of the first of these mills was the Ballantine grist mill at Grassmere on the north side of Peninsula Lake. Owned by a canny Scot named Robert Ballantine, who arranged for many local settlers to contribute to its construction, the mill operated from 1875 to 1895 at the lower cascade on Ballantine's Creek. This modest mill, powered by a waterwheel, was an important social gathering place in addition to its normal function. But it never made Ballantine a rich man. It was customary in Muskoka, and elsewhere, for farmers to pay the miller not with cash (which they didn't have anyway) but with one twelfth of the flour produced from their grain (sawmill owners, however, would keep one half of a settler's logs in exchange for sawing the other half into lumber). Declining business finally closed the Ballantine grist mill.

Not far from Grassmere, at the outlet of Walker Lake,

THE LOCKS (COTTRILL) MILL, 1954. *In this view down the river you can see the government control dam at the head of the rapids and, on the left side of the mill, the entrance to the canal leading to the Huntsville Lock.*
· Ministry of Natural Resources

another Scot, Robert Walker, built a water-powered sawmill and grist mill soon after arriving with his family and taking up Free Grant lots there in 1876. The sawmill operation continued until the 1920s. Remains of the mill foundation, turbine, penstock and the old grist mill stones lie in the bush at the foot of a cliff where Walker Lake spills from a quiet cedar- and hemlock-fringed bay.

One of the most interesting mill sites in northern Muskoka was at the Hoodstown Rapids, where the Buck River tumbles from Fox Lake down into Lake Vernon. It's possible that Free Grant settler William Haney built a small water-powered sawmill and grist mill there as early as 1872, but the real story revolves around the activities of Charles Hood and his wife Janet. They came north to Muskoka and in 1874 purchased the land all around the rapids, apparently impressed with its potential as a village site. A small settlement did begin to grow beside Charles' dam and water-powered sawmill near the top of the rapids. It was named Port Vernon in 1877, the year the new steamboat *Northern* began to ply between it and Port Sydney, and then renamed Hoodstown in 1879. At that time the settlement boasted three general stores, two churches, a hotel and a dozen or more homes, and rumours had begun to fly that the railway might come through the village when it was extended north from Gravenhurst. In 1880 Janet Hood filed subdivision plans for Hoodstown and over 100 lots were sold, many apparently to speculators who hoped to make a quick profit when the railway arrived and land values soared.

But the railway never came. Residents of the little village of Huntsville, at the east end of Lake Vernon, lobbied vigorously, and successfully, in favour of a more easterly route for the railway through their community. After the new railway opened for business in 1886, Hoodstown rapidly declined. The post office closed in 1891, and the Hoods moved back to Toronto. By the turn of the century it had become another ghost town.

Northwest of Hoodstown, near the hamlet of Yearley, a water-powered sawmill operated for many years at a cascade on Axe Creek, largest tributary of the Buck River. Stisted Township pioneer James Campbell may have built the first little mill there in the late 1870s. In the early 1890s Lorenzo Howell re-established the operation, a little backwoods sawmill equipped with grist-mill stones as well and powered by an overshot waterwheel (a turbine may have been installed later). The Howell mill survived until the 1920s.

On the north side of Lake Vernon, near the hamlet of Ravenscliffe, a small water-powered grist mill served local farmers for a few years in the 1870s and 1880s. By means of an overshot waterwheel it harnessed a steep cascade on a tiny creek a few hundred metres from the lake. It was built by James Sharpe or John Piper.

A little further north, on what would become known as Jessop's Creek, James Jacob Jessop built a water-powered sawmill about 1875. He relied on a dam to create a head of water, as there were only minor rapids at the mill site. The mill didn't last very long; the next spring flood took out the dam. Although Jessop himself apparently didn't rebuild, some evidence suggests that others subsequently did.

Settlers made a couple of attempts in the 1880s to establish water mills (primarily sawmills) on Black Creek, a western tributary to Lake Vernon in Stisted Township not far from Hoodstown. One didn't work properly, the other lasted until the next spring freshet took it out (as Stisted pioneer W.H. Demaine wryly noted, Stisted mills produced more experience than lumber).

No doubt the pioneers made other attempts to build and operate water mills in the Muskoka River watershed in the late 19th century. In that era people regarded water power in much the same way we today regard diesel engines and electric motors — a pretty ordinary way of running machinery.

Nobody really realized the historical importance of the water mills until they were gone. That in large measure explains why only a few ruins, and often nothing at all, remains of the Muskoka River mills which once played such an important role in the pioneer economy.

THE END OF AN ERA. *The Locks Mill, last operating water-powered sawmill on the Muskoka River system, was seriously disabled not long before this 1954 photograph. Part of the mill collapsed due to a washout of the wall of the canal leading to the lock. The canal, on the left, has been blocked off pending repairs to the wall.* · Ministry of Natural Resources

LOWER BRACEBRIDGE FALLS GENERATING STATION, c. 1904. From 1902 to 1906 the station was equipped with just one generator and penstock (water pipeline). The small cottage over the headworks at the top was added later.

· Archives of Ontario Acc. 15963-9

CHAPTER 9

Water into Watts: Hydroelectricity from the Muskoka River

When the pioneers moved north into the hills and forests of Muskoka, many of them soon took advantage of one of the Muskoka River's most valuable assets: the water-power potential of its numerous falls and rapids. They harnessed this power to run mills, just as civilizations elsewhere had been doing for 2,000 years.

But at the time settlement began in the Muskoka watershed, steam power was rapidly becoming the prime mover of industry, and within a few decades electric motors and then internal combustion engines began to further displace the waterwheel and hydraulic turbine for direct industrial power. The water-mill era was fast drawing to a close.

Despite these changes, water power wasn't destined to fade from the scene. In the waning years of the 19th century a new use for water power began to emerge, one that would lead to the harnessing of waterfalls on the Muskoka and other rivers on an unprecedented scale. Water power had been found ideally suited to the generation of electricity.

Electricity had been studied and experimented with for a long time, but not until the 1870s were the first practical applications made, when a few mills and factories in the United States and Europe installed small generators to power carbon-arc lights. This type of light, however, was not suited to large-scale commercial and residential use, thus the demand for electricity remained small. The perfection of the incandescent light bulb in 1880 quickly changed all that. Sud-denly a huge potential market for electric lighting existed. Electrical generating and transmission technology galloped forward in the coming years, further spurred by the increasing use of electric motors. Industries, private electric companies and municipalities began to build electric generation stations and string power lines along the streets.

Both steam engines and hydraulic turbines were used to spin electric generators. The turbine, in general use since 1850 to power mill machinery, was well suited to the task of turning a generator. Water-powered electric generating stations (hydroelectric stations) sprang up at waterfalls in or near towns, and at more remote ones as transmission technology improved. Because the electric power line meant that the energy didn't have to be used at the waterfalls, as was the case with water mills, the full potential of large waterfalls could be tapped, as well as that of waterfalls unsuited for mills due to inconvenient location or difficult terrain.

Although some mills connected small generators to waterwheels or turbines in the 1870s to provide for their own lighting, the world's first true hydroelectric station opened in 1882 at Appleton, Wisconsin. Just ten years after that the first hydroelectric station began operating on the Muskoka River. By 1950 eleven stations tapped the energy of ten waterfalls on the river. Ten of these, with a total capacity of about 27,000 kilowatts, operate today. Hydroelectric development had similarly burgeoned across Canada. At present about two thirds of the country's electricity comes from the energy of falling water. Up until the 1960s hydroelectric stations provided nearly all of Ontario's electric power.

You may have seen a few of the Muskoka River hydroelectric stations humming away amid the rock and pine of the Canadian Shield. They probably strike you as tiny and insignificant compared to the huge power stations that now feed most of the electricity into the province-wide grid of transmission lines, but for many years they generated virtually all of Muskoka's electricity and significant amounts for communities to the south. Prior to the Second World War, electric systems were not extensively interconnected in Ontario; each region had to rely on its own water-power resources. In those days the little Muskoka River plants were as vital as the big Sir Adam Beck station at Niagara Falls. Even today we should not scoff at their output: each year they generate over 150,000,000 kilowatt-hours of electricity, enough to supply 12,000 homes.

Electricity in Ontario is almost synonymous with the big provincial utility, Ontario Hydro, formed in 1906 (as the Hydro-Electric Power Commission of Ontario) to supply power at cost to municipalities. Until 1906, and even for some years afterwards, private firms and municipalities took the initiative in hydroelectric generation. That was the case on the Muskoka River. Ontario Hydro didn't acquire its first Muskoka River plant until 1915; after that it greatly expanded its generation capacity on the river, becoming by far the largest producer of electricity in Muskoka. Today, Ontario Hydro owns five of the ten major hydroelectric stations on the Muskoka River, accounting for 80 percent of the installed capacity. The Town of Bracebridge owns three, the City of Orillia one. Marsh Hydropower Inc. operates another in a powerhouse owned by Muskoka Lakes Township. There is also one small private facility providing power for an isolated homestead.

EARLY HYDROELECTRIC DEVELOPMENT ON THE MUSKOKA RIVER

It's hardly surprising that the town of Bracebridge became the site of the pioneering hydroelectric development in the Muskoka watershed back in 1892; powerful Bracebridge Falls roared through the heart of the community and had been supporting important water mills for three decades. When in 1889 the new town council began investigating the possibility of replacing the existing kerosene street lamps with electric lights, it was inevitable that the power would come from the falls. The only question was, who would provide it?

Initially Bracebridge contracted with the Ball Electric Light Company to provide the service. The Ball firm planned to build a hydroelectric station at the falls. Unfortunately, it never did so, and by 1892 the town still didn't have any electricity. That year help came from a different source. A man named William Sutherland Shaw built a small 60-kilowatt hydro station at the top of the falls, beside the Bird Woollen Mill, to supply electricity to the town's newest tannery (Shaw was the tannery manager). Bracebridge negotiated with Shaw to provide the electric street-lighting from his plant, the first hydroelectric station in Muskoka.*

* It's possible that Henry Bird actually generated the first hydroelectricity from the Muskoka River. Certain evidence suggests that in the 1880s he connected a small generator to the turbine in his woollen mill at Bracebridge Falls. It produced current to run lights in his nearby residence, Woodchester Villa, and probably in the mill as well.

PIONEER HYDRO. This hydroelectric station at Upper Bracebridge Falls was the very first in the Muskoka River watershed. At the time of this photograph (early 1900s) it served Bracebridge as both electric-generating and water-pumping station. The Bird Woollen Mill stands immediately to the left.

- Ken Veitch/Town of Bracebridge

BIRD'S MILL PUMPING STATION, 1987. In somewhat altered but still recognizable form, this is the original pumping and generating station at Upper Bracebridge Falls. It still pumps water for Bracebridge.

It's clear that Bracebridge considered the arrangement with Shaw only a temporary one. What the town really had in mind was a municipally-owned station to generate electricity not only for street-lighting, but, for the first time, for residential and commercial lighting as well. That objective became a reality in 1894 when, after failing to attract satisfactory bids to build a new plant, the town bought Shaw's plant for $3,500.

By that purchase Bracebridge became the first Ontario municipality to own and operate its own hydroelectric station as a public utility — certainly a tribute to the far-sightedness of the local politicians and rate-payers at that time. Bracebridge went on to become one of the few lasting success stories in the field of municipal hydroelectric generation. Of the dozens of towns that built or purchased hydro stations afterwards, only 11 in Ontario, including Bracebridge, still operate them.

In 1895 Bracebridge installed a larger turbine and generator in its new plant to meet the increased demand for lighting from businesses and residences. The following year it connected the original turbine to a pump to supply the new municipal waterworks system. As the decade wore on, the demand for electricity continued to rise. The town council no doubt perceived that with the development of practical electric motors a potentially large market existed for industrial electric power too. An abundant supply of inexpensive hydroelectricity would give any town an edge in attracting and retaining industry. So, in 1900 Bracebridge embarked on a much larger and bolder hydroelectric project at the falls.

The new scheme involved the construction of a second powerhouse at the foot of the falls to utilize the entire drop of about 10.7 metres (35 feet) below the tailraces of the Bird Woollen Mill and the original powerhouse. The first generator, rated at 300 kilowatts, went into service in 1902, a second one of the same capacity in 1906. Still in service today, the charming stone plant is one of the oldest operating hydroelectric stations in Canada.

After the town installed the second generator, in 1906, it removed the generator from the old upper falls plant and replaced it with another water pump, powered by the turbine. Thereafter that plant served solely as a municipal water-pumping station, a function it still serves to this day. Although electric pumps installed in 1914 do the work now, the original water-powered equipment was used regularly until 1959 and is still available for emergency use.

After Bracebridge Falls, the next waterfall in the Muskoka watershed to undergo hydroelectric development was the largest one, South Falls. Conveniently located between Bracebridge and Gravenhurst, it sparked a rivalry between those two towns, as both sought to obtain the rights to develop it.

The town of Gravenhurst became interested in hydroelectric development in the early 1900s. It already owned a steam-powered generating station, but of course electricity from such a facility was more expensive due to the cost of fuel. So, in 1905 the town began investigating the nearby large waterfalls along the South Muskoka River. For possible hydro development Gravenhurst liked South Falls best, as it was the biggest, but because Bracebridge wanted that one to meet its own future power needs, Gravenhurst decided in 1906 to harness Trethewey Falls instead.

Then, abruptly, the town reversed its decision and began competing with Bracebridge for the valuable South Falls power lease. After Bracebridge refused a joint development, the Ontario government quickly awarded the lease to Graven-

PICTURESQUE HYDRO. *Still generating electricity today, the attractive stone plant at Lower Bracebridge Falls is one of the oldest operating hydroelectric stations in Canada. It began service in 1902.*

ORIGINAL SOUTH FALLS GENERATING STATION. *The Town of Gravenhurst built this tiny plant at the foot of the falls in 1907. The large wooden trough to the left of the powerhouse is the end of the slide that carried logs past the falls.*

· Ontario Hydro

WILSON'S FALLS GENERATING STATION, 1986. *Owned by Bracebridge, its appearance has changed very little since it was built in 1910. The dam behind the powerhouse impounds a head pond on a secondary channel of the falls. The main falls is out of sight to the right.*

hurst, and in 1907 the town built the original South Falls generating station. The 360-kilowatt generator, housed in a little red-brick cottage at the foot of the falls, tapped but a fraction of the energy of the mighty cataract. Water for the turbine came through a steel pipeline that ran over 305 metres (1,000 feet) from the top of the falls.

Unsuccessful in its bid for South Falls, Bracebridge turned its eyes northward and secured the power rights to nearby Wilson's Falls and High Falls on the North Muskoka River. Rising electrical demands forced the town to begin construction of a hydroelectric station at Wilson's Falls in 1909 to supplement the Bracebridge Falls station. Completed in 1910 at a cost of $52,000, a new plant produced 600 kilowatts from a single generator. It still operates today, drawing its water from a dam and head pond on a secondary channel that bypasses the main falls — the same channel harnessed by the old Norwood Mills.

With both Gravenhurst and Bracebridge enjoying the benefits of hydroelectric power, it was hardly surprising that Muskoka's third major town, Huntsville, decided to replace its steam-powered plant with a water-powered one. In 1908 the northern town began seriously looking for a suitable waterfall to develop; like Gravenhurst, it had no waterfall within the town limits. As the power question dragged on over the next several years, engineers hired by the town or provided by Ontario Hydro examined waterfalls on the North and South Muskoka, the Big East, Buck and Oxtongue rivers.

A hydroelectric scheme initially favoured by many didn't involve a waterfalls at all. Known as the Portage Scheme, it centred on an interesting accident of geography a few kilometres east of Huntsville where Peninsula Lake approaches to within a kilometre of Lake of Bays, but lies at an elevation 31.4 metres (103 feet) lower. The idea was to divert some Lake of Bays water through a canal and 579-metre-long (1,900-foot) tunnel to a powerhouse on Peninsula Lake.

Unfortunately, that meant taking water out of the South Muskoka River system and putting it into the North Muskoka, and that didn't sit well with some interests. Gravenhurst didn't want any reduction of flows at South Falls, lumber companies feared less water in the South Muskoka would hinder their log drives, and steamboat and resort operators on Lake of Bays thought the lake level might be adversely affected. The government officially scuttled the Portage Scheme in 1913.

Long before that, however, other sites had come under serious consideration, notably Ragged Falls on the Oxtongue River and High Falls on the North Muskoka (Huntsville's interest in the latter raised the ire of Bracebridge and caused considerable friction between the two towns). But one by one these and other waterfalls were rejected as being too remote, too costly to develop, or possessing insufficient power potential to meet Huntsville's existing and future electrical needs.

In 1910 Huntsville began showing serious interest in buying hydroelectric power from Gravenhurst's South Falls development. Although Gravenhurst expressed a willingness to sell power to Huntsville, negotiations between the two towns went nowhere. That, combined with Huntsville's failure to find another waterfall it considered suitable, led to the South Falls power question being placed in the hands of Ontario Hydro in 1911.

It was becoming increasingly clear that South Falls held the

SOUTH FALLS GENERATING STATION, May 1924. Reno-
vations and additions made in 1915-16 by Ontario Hydro completely
changed the appearance of the original Gravenhurst plant. Work on a
second expansion was just getting under way at the time of this photograph. Note the water gushing down the log slide. The annual spring
log drive was in progress.   · Ontario Hydro

key to meeting the future electrical needs not only of Huntsville but, because of its enormous power potential, of all of
Muskoka. Gravenhurst, however, held the water-power lease
there and unfortunately did not have the resources to undertake a major expansion of its little generating station. And
much to Huntsville's annoyance, Ontario Hydro did not move
quickly at all to find a satisfactory solution to the problem.
Finally, the situation came to a head in 1915. Ontario Hydro
had signed a contract with Huntsville to supply the town
with hydroelectricity within 18 months. South Falls was the
only practical place to generate the amount required. So, in
the summer of 1915 the provincial utility negotiated the take-
over of the South Falls generating station and power lease
from Gravenhurst. The town still owed a great deal of
money on the plant and was only too happy to be relieved
of the burden.

Immediately upon acquiring the South Falls generating station — only its fourth plant at that time — Ontario Hydro
began renovating and expanding it in order to supply both
Gravenhurst and Huntsville. A second turbine and generator
were added, the latter rated at 635 kilowatts. The new unit
began operating in the late summer of 1916, with power
deliveries to Huntsville commencing at that time over a new
42-kilometre (26-mile) transmission line. After an eight-year
struggle Huntsville finally had its hydroelectricity.

While the work at South Falls progressed, a private company was making plans for a smaller but locally significant
hydroelectric development on the west side of Lake Muskoka at Bala. Members of Bala's founding Burgess family
(notably Dr. Alexander Burgess, son of Thomas Burgess and
first mayor of Bala) had formed the Bala Electric Light and
Power Company to harness the energy of Bala Falls. In 1917

the company built a 100-kilowatt hydroelectric plant on the Millstream, on the site where nearly half a century earlier Thomas Burgess built his water-powered sawmill.

Serving only Bala at first, the company subsequently ran lines to Port Carling and MacTier, and in 1922 added a second generator, of 90 kilowatts capacity, to meet the increased demand. A second powerhouse, equipped with one 250-kilowatt generator, was built on the middle channel of Bala Falls in 1924.

The Bala Electric Light and Power Company was typical of scores of small private firms established in the late 1800s and early 1900s to generate and sell electricity to communities across the province. Most found it difficult after a few years to maintain and expand service, and they were taken over by Ontario Hydro. The Bala company sold out to Ontario Hydro in 1929. By that time the provincial utility was well into a major expansion of its hydroelectric generating capacity in the Muskoka River watershed.

THE BIG HYDROELECTRIC EXPANSION, 1924-1941

Although the Muskoka River system possesses a water-power potential in excess of 75,000 kilowatts, the comparatively small and dispersed population of Muskoka District did not readily lead to the harnessing of a significant part of that resource to generate electricity. By 1924, 32 years after the first hydroelectric station opened at Bracebridge Falls, the river supported just five small hydro stations, which boasted a combined capacity of less than 3,000 kilowatts and served only six towns and villages and a couple of hamlets.

The next 17 years, however, would see a startling ninefold increase in hydroelectric capacity on the Muskoka River. This

BALA NO. 2 GENERATING STATION, *Bala Falls, 1952.*
You can't visit this one anymore. It was torn down in 1972. The middle channel of Bala Falls tumbles just to the left, beyond this view. · Ontario Hydro B3749

huge expansion was carried out entirely by Ontario Hydro. Increased demand for electricity in Gravenhurst and Huntsville, plus the extension of Ontario Hydro power lines to smaller villages and rural areas of Muskoka, necessitated some of this activity. To a large degree, however, the expansion was fuelled by steadily rising power requirements to the south of Muskoka.

When Ontario Hydro acquired the South Falls generating station from Gravenhurst in 1915, it did so with the intention of ultimately enlarging it to tap a far greater proportion of the immense power potential of South Falls. Even with a modest initial expansion completed in 1916 to serve Huntsville, scarcely a tenth of that potential had been realized. By the early 1920s, with the generators straining to carry the growing electrical loads in Huntsville and Gravenhurst, and the demand for electricity continuing to grow to the south, Ontario Hydro began to make preparations for a major expansion at South Falls and a transmission line to send the surplus power southward.

Work on Phase 1 of the South Falls expansion began in 1924. Over the next year Ontario Hydro removed the original turbine, generator and water pipeline installed by Gravenhurst in 1907, then built new pipelines to supply two bigger turbines and generators, the latter rated at 1,600 kilowatts each. The new units were placed in service in 1925. They brought the rated plant capacity up to 3,835 kilowatts, the same as it is today.

The new transmission line to the south was also completed in 1925. It electrically connected Muskoka with southern Ontario for the first time. The Muskoka System (comprising the South Falls station, Huntsville and Gravenhurst) became the Muskoka Division of Ontario Hydro's new Georgian Bay System, which, in addition to Muskoka, encompassed a large area around Lake Simcoe and southern Georgian Bay. At that time three other Ontario Hydro generating stations — two on the Severn River and one on the Beaver — also served the Georgian Bay System. Interestingly, these were the first three stations built or acquired by Ontario Hydro. South Falls was the fourth (or third, it may be argued, since the Beaver River plant, under construction before the South Falls purchase, didn't go into service until shortly afterwards).

Phase 2 of the South Falls expansion got under way in 1925. It involved the construction of a combined dam and powerhouse just a few hundred metres upstream from South Falls, at the Hanna Chutes. Power generation was just a beneficial spin-off from this project; its prime purpose was to create a large head pond, or reservoir, to handle daily fluctuations in the demand for water at the enlarged South Falls station. The dam, wedged between sheer rock walls at the foot of the Hanna Chutes, raised the water level 9.8 metres (32 feet), enough to drown out the chutes behind and flood the river back into Spence Lake above. A single 1,120-kilowatt generator in the powerhouse began service in 1926.

Just two years later Ontario Hydro began building a dam and powerhouse at Trethewey Falls, the next waterfall up the South Muskoka. This 1,600-kilowatt hydroelectric station was rushed to completion in 1929 to meet the growing electrical demand in the Georgian Bay System. Both the Trethewey Falls and Hanna Chute stations were run by remote control from South Falls. Remote control technology made it feasible to operate small plants like these. Today all of Ontario Hydro's generating stations in the Muskoka watershed are remote-controlled from the Essa Transformer Station near Barrie.

SOUTH FALLS GENERATING STATION (*final version*). *The 1924-25 expansion brought the plant to its present size and appearance. Three wood stave pipelines carry water 308 metres (1,010 feet) from the top of the falls to the turbines in the powerhouse. The bridges at the top carry Highway 11 across the South Falls gorge.*

HANNA CHUTE GENERATING STATION, 1929. *Wedged into the Lower Hanna Chute gorge, the development originally incorporated a short log slide to by-pass the dam. The front of the powerhouse has now been faced with aluminum siding.*

· Ontario Hydro

TRETHEWEY FALLS GENERATING STATION, *1932.* The powerhouse blocks a small secondary channel of the falls. The dam, which also extends across the main channel of the falls (out of sight behind and to the right) necessitated the log slide here too.

· Ontario Hydro HP·1540

Although Ontario Hydro selected four sites for possible hydroelectric installations on the South Muskoka River between Hanna Chute and Baysville, it actually developed only Trethewey Falls. The relatively modest potential of these sites was considered insufficient to meet the projected growth in electricity consumption in the Georgian Bay System. Even as Ontario Hydro installed generators on the South Muskoka in the 1920s it was already shifting its attention to far greater water-power resources in the western part of the watershed.

West of Lake Muskoka huge quantities of water rushed down the Moon and Musquash rivers to Georgian Bay, falling 48.5 metres (159 feet) in a fairly short distance over numerous falls and rapids. The two tiny hydroelectric stations at Bala Falls (purchased by Ontario Hydro in 1929) harnessed less than two percent of the estimated 30,000-kilowatt potential of these rivers. Clearly the lower reaches of the Muskoka River system could meet the electrical needs of customers in the Georgian Bay System for many years to come.

As a result of studies it conducted in the 1920s, Ontario Hydro evolved a bold scheme to harness the Moon and Musquash. It would divert most of the flow of the Moon into the Musquash and, as the need arose, build four hydroelectric stations on the latter (a new, larger plant at Bala Falls was also contemplated). In those days the ecological consequences of such a diversion didn't enter into the equation. Power utilities regarded rivers primarily as convenient canals to be dammed and altered at will. So did the lumbermen, who for many years had diverted the Moon to aid their Musquash River log drives.

Work on the first Musquash River power station, at Ragged Rapids, about six kilometres (3.7 miles) below Bala,

was originally slated to begin in 1929. The onset of the Great Depression, however, delayed it for several years (during which time the power wasn't required) and construction of the $1.2 million project didn't get under way until 1937. The development consisted of two main elements: a combined dam and powerhouse at the foot of the Ragged Rapids gorge, and a diversion dam nearby on the Moon River. These completely drowned out Ragged Rapids as well as the Moon Chutes just upstream, creating a drop of 11.3 metres (37 feet) for the turbines.

In the autumn of 1938 the two generators in the powerhouse, rated at a total of 7,650 kilowatts, began feeding current into the system. Some idea of the importance of the Ragged Rapids station is evident when you consider that when it opened it produced nearly as much power as all the other hydroelectric stations on the Muskoka River combined and represented 30 percent of the generating capacity in the Georgian Bay System. Most of its output initially went south out of Muskoka along a transmission line built a few years earlier.

As a result of the burgeoning electrical demands of wartime industry, Ontario Hydro had to begin work on the second Musquash River power station in 1940. The new development, completed the following year, was located at Big Eddy, eight kilometres (5 miles) downstream from Ragged Rapids. About half of the 11-metre (36-foot) head of water came from the Big Eddy chute, the rest from a 122-metre-long (400-foot) dam thrown across the river a little further upstream. The dam created a large reservoir that inundated several minor rapids. An artificial canal led water from the reservoir to the powerhouse on the edge of the Big Eddy plunge pool. The two generators installed at Big Eddy

RAGGED RAPIDS GENERATING STATION. A combined dam and powerhouse at the foot of the old Ragged Rapids gorge completely inundates the rough set of chutes that spilled down through the forests here prior to 1938. Ragged Rapids was the highest waterfall on the Musquash River.

· Ontario Hydro 3445·5

Big Eddy Devp. 196.
Generator Room from Gallery at South end.

Oct. 26. 1943.

GENERATOR ROOM, Big Eddy Powerhouse. The two generators are each rated at 3,825 kilowatts. Connected by vertical shafts to a pair of 5,280-horsepower turbines below, they spin at 200 r.p.m. and together generate nearly 40,000,000 kilowatt-hours of electricity each year, on average.

· Ontario Hydro

have the same capacity as those at Ragged Rapids (7,650 kilowatts).

Big Eddy, as it turned out, was the last power station Ontario Hydro built in the Muskoka River system.

THE DECLINE AND REVIVAL OF HYDROELECTRICITY

Up until the early 1940s Ontario Hydro met the electrical needs of many parts of the province by building relatively small hydroelectric stations on nearby rivers. Developments on the Muskoka, Severn and Beaver rivers to serve the Georgian Bay area illustrate this strategy perfectly. In the 1940s, however, the utility accelerated a large-scale integration of its various power systems across southern Ontario and began to rely exclusively on very large power stations built on major rivers, and later on thermal-electric stations, to meet escalating post-war electricity consumption. It was no longer considered economically viable to build small hydroelectric stations that could generate only a few thousand kilowatts.

Ontario Hydro not only stopped building small stations such as those on the Muskoka River, but closed some of the existing ones down. The two little Bala Falls plants didn't produce any more power after 1957. Unfortunately, in an era of mega-projects, 450 kilowatts didn't seem worth bothering about. The Middle Falls station was torn down in 1972. The Millstream plant, however, has been put back to work, but not by Ontario Hydro. More about that shortly.

The smaller water-power sites still interested some of the municipal electric utilities in Ontario. Both Bracebridge and Orillia built new hydroelectric stations on the Muskoka River shortly after the war to insure a few more years independence from the Ontario Hydro system. Bracebridge, through

its Power, Light and Water Commission, already operated plants at Bracebridge Falls and Wilson's Falls. When the generators in these began to prove inadequate, work started in 1947 on a $228,000 development at High Falls on the North Muskoka River. The town had wisely obtained the power lease for that site in 1907 against the day when it would require an additional source of electricity. Opened in 1948, the modest 800-kilowatt High Falls station brought the town's total generating capacity up to 2,000 kilowatts.

In 1949 construction began on the Orillia Water Light and Power Commission's million-dollar hydroelectric development at Matthiasville on the South Muskoka. This project featured a huge 269-metre-long (882-foot) concrete dam spanning the valley near the top of Matthias Falls. It created a total drop of 13.4 metres (44 feet) down to the turbine in the powerhouse below and formed a lake extending 3.3 kilometres (2 miles) upstream. The single 2,812-kilowatt generator began feeding power into a 64-kilometre (40-mile) transmission line to Orillia in 1950.

Orillia, like Bracebridge, had long been involved in municipal hydroelectric generation. It built a power station at Ragged Rapids on the Severn River in 1901, replacing that in 1917 with a 3,600-kilowatt facility at Swift Rapids further downstream. The town added another 3,600-kilowatt plant in 1935 near Minden, on the Gull River. Preliminary studies and land acquisition proceedings for the Matthiasville development got under way in 1945. Ontario Hydro had studied this site in the 1920s but no longer considered it important for its own needs.

The Matthiasville station was the last major hydroelectric development in the Muskoka watershed. In the 1950s both Bracebridge and Orillia were forced by power shortages to

MATTHIASVILLE DAM, *South Muskoka River. In this view from the road bridge you can see only the central part of this huge barrier. A penstock (out of sight to the left) carries water to the powerhouse at the foot of the falls.*

MATTHIASVILLE GENERATING STATION. *The 3,770-horsepower Kaplan turbine in the powerhouse can gulp the entire average flow of the South Muskoka River. This station is run by remote control from Orillia.*

join the Ontario Hydro system. Since then Bracebridge has been content to maintain its three North Muskoka River stations, which actually harness only a small part of the energy of their respective waterfalls. The proportion of the town's annual energy requirements met by these stations has steadily fallen to about 40 percent (1985) — nonetheless, the highest proportion among those Ontario municipalities that still run their own hydroelectric plants.

Orillia has been more ambitious. In addition to more than doubling the capacity of its Swift Rapids plant, it actively investigated several more waterfalls on the Muskoka River for possible hydroelectric development. Sites at Crozier's Rapids and Slater's Chute on the South Muskoka above Matthiasville were rejected in 1970 on economic grounds, but in 1978 Orillia was poised to proceed with two larger hydroelectric stations on the Musquash River: an 8,000-kilowatt plant at Sandy Gray's Chute, and one of 6,700 kilowatts at Go Home Chute. These were the two remaining sites Ontario Hydro had originally planned to develop on the Musquash.

The schemes Orillia proposed differed little from those conceived back in the 1920s by Ontario Hydro when there were no cottages in the area and little public awareness of ecological impacts. Circumstances and attitudes had changed by the 1970s. The government required an environmental impact assessment before it could approve the projects. That assessment revealed potential problems arising largely from the plan to divert most of the outflow from Go Home Lake down the Go Home River rather than the Musquash and to virtually by-pass Flat Rock Lake entirely.

Hundreds of cottagers on Go Home Lake reacted vehemently against the projects. Among other things they cited the potential ecological problems (destruction of fish spawning beds, possible water quality deterioration in Go Home Lake), the drowning of scenic waterfalls, and the loss of the wilderness character of the area. Orillia concluded that it would never get the necessary government approval and abandoned its plans for the new generating stations.

There still exists in the Muskoka River system a substantial reserve of untapped water-power potential that we could put to work generating electricity without spoiling the beauty of waterfalls or incurring destructive ecological consequences. In fact, all across the settled parts of Ontario literally hundreds of modest waterfalls and old mill dams could supply us with in excess of a quarter of a million kilowatts of power. Water power is non-polluting, renewable and, insofar as the fuel is concerned, free. It is a wise alternative to burning coal or splitting atoms, an alternative we would be irresponsible not to use whenever possible. And what could better symbolize the wise use of Nature's wealth than a small hydroelectric station designed with care to blend with the rock and pine and the tumbling waters of a falls?

Happily, the small hydroelectric station is now slowly regaining popularity. A more favourable government attitude and the introduction of innovative standardized turbine-generator units has made it somewhat easier to develop or redevelop small hydro sites at a reasonable cost, although many bureaucratic obstacles need yet to be removed. Modest hydroelectric stations would fit in well at such sites on the Muskoka River as the Huntsville Lock dam, Port Sydney Falls, Balsam Chute, the Baysville Dam, Bala Falls, the Go Home Lake dam, as well as at many smaller waterfalls that could be developed for private domestic, farm or industrial use.

In addition, some partially developed water-power sites provide potential for expansion. The Town of Bracebridge, for instance, would find it advantageous to add a second generator at both its Wilson's Falls and High Falls power stations, and possibly consider returning the Bird's Mill Pumping Station to its original hydroelectric function (the Bird's Mill Pumping Station, as the facility is now known, is actually the original powerhouse built in 1892 by W.S. Shaw).

At least one resident of Muskoka has taken his own initiative in developing small-scale hydro. In 1985 John Fiorini of Shannon Hall, Cardwell Township, installed a 15-kilowatt generating plant at a waterfall on the Rosseau River. The little home-built facility supplies power for the isolated Fiorini homestead. In a way Mr. Fiorini has rekindled the spirit of the hard-working pioneers who originally tapped the Muskoka River waterfalls to run their little frontier mills. Now a few other Muskoka residents are considering small hydro projects too.

In 1987 another positive step was taken when Muskoka Lakes Township decided to re-activate the historic Millstream (Bala No. 1) generating station at Bala Falls. The township had acquired the inoperative plant and associated dam some years earlier. Faced with the prospect of having to spend a large sum to repair or demolish the deteriorating structure, it decided instead to lease the plant to a private company that would agree to fix it up and run it as a business venture.

Marsh Hydropower Inc., a Port Colborne firm that specializes in small hydro developments, put forward the most satisfactory plan to refurbish the Bala generating station and it was awarded the lease. In 1988-89 the company repaired the powerhouse and dam, rehabilitated the old turbines, and installed two new 125-kilowatt generators. It sells the power produced to Ontario Hydro. Fittingly, the rejuvenated facility is officially known as the Burgess Generating Station.

Hopefully in the years to come more small hydroelectric stations will be installed to tap some of the remaining unharnessed energy of the Muskoka River. Turning water into watts doesn't have to compromise scenic beauty or natural ecosystems. Past practice to the contrary must serve as a lesson, not as a deterrent.

FORMER HYDROELECTRIC STATIONS, MUSKOKA RIVER

Station and Owner	Head of water metres	Main Generators	
		Years in Service	Rated power kilowatts
Bracebridge Falls (Upper Falls) Town of Bracebridge[1]	5.0	1892-1895	60
		1895-1906	93
Bala No. 2 Ontario Hydro[2]	5.8	1924-1960	250

[1] Purchased from W.S. Shaw in 1894. Turbines used to run water pumps after generators removed.
[2] Purchased from Bala Electric Light and Power Company in 1929. Plant officially closed in 1960 but produced little or no power after 1957.

OPERATING HYDROELECTRIC STATIONS, MUSKOKA RIVER

Station and Owner	Head of water metres	Main Generators		Station and Owner	Head of water metres	Main Generators	
		Year Installed	Rated power kilowatts			Year Installed	Rated power kilowatts
Bracebridge Falls (Lower Falls) Bracebridge Hydro	10.7	1902 1906	300 300 600	Ragged Rapids Ontario Hydro	11.3	1938 1938	3,825 3,825 7,650
Wilson's Falls Bracebridge Hydro	12.5	1910	600	Big Eddy Ontario Hydro	11.0	1941 1941	3,825 3,825 7,650
High Falls Bracebridge Hydro	14.6	1948	800	Matthiasville Orillia WLPC	13.4	1950	2,812
South Falls Ontario Hydro[1]	33.2	(1907) 1916 1925 1925	(360) 635 1,600 1,600 3,835	Rosseau River John Fiorini	9.0	1985	15
Hanna Chute Ontario Hydro	9.8	1926	1,120	Bala No. 1 (Millstream) Muskoka Lakes Tp[2]	5.3	(1917) (1922) 1989 1989	(100) (90)[3] 125 125 250
Trethewey Falls Ontario Hydro	10.7	1929	1,600				26,932

[1] Purchased from Town of Gravenhurst in 1915.

[2] Originally owned by Bala Electric Light and Power Co.; Purchased by Ontario Hydro in 1929; inoperative 1957-1988. Operated now by Marsh Hydropower Inc. under lease from Tp.

[3] Replaced in 1929 by a 120-kW unit.

TRANQUIL MORNING ON FAIRY LAKE. *A backdrop of rolling wooded hills lends a subdued air of remoteness to the lakes throughout the eastern half of the Muskoka watershed.*

CHAPTER 10

A Land of Lakes: Steamboat Navigation and the Rise of Resorts and Tourism

Viewed from the perspective of the hawk circling high overhead, the countryside drained by the Muskoka River stretches off to the far horizon as an endless vista of forests and lakes. You don't begin to appreciate how much water there is until you gaze down from the skies. In all directions you see lakes and ponds strewn recklessly across the landscape, tranquil gems nestled in the hollows, elongated fingers outstretched between rocky ridges, sprawling expanses of blue waters dotted with green islands, all of them sparkling and shimmering in the sun.

If you possessed the time and patience you could count all of these lakes. Although the largest dozen or so dominate the scene, you would nonetheless find some 500 in all that exceed 10 hectares (25 acres), and you would still be counting at 1,600, including small ponds. Altogether lakes and ponds cover about 675 square kilometres (260 square miles), or nearly one seventh of the entire Muskoka River watershed (and that doesn't include extensive areas of marsh and other wetland). Little wonder, then, that lakes figure so prominently in our perception of Muskoka, little wonder that lakes have played such an important role in the history of the district.

Back in the pioneer days of the 19th century the big lakes in the central and western parts of the Muskoka River system played a pivotal role in encouraging settlement, industry

and tourism. Steamboats plying these waters provided fast, comfortable and inexpensive transportation across the otherwise rocky and densely wooded Canadian Shield, where roads were little more than rutted trails. Of course the great beauty and tremendous recreational opportunities of the lakes also helped stimulate the growth of tourism and continue to support this booming industry that has long been the heart of the Muskoka economy.

In short, the natural advantages of the Muskoka River's lakes, especially the big lakes, helped Muskoka flourish in the early years and then survive the subsequent decline of farming and lumbering, which, in the absence of tourism, would have severely crippled the economy. We must not forget either that the lakes form the basis of the water regulation mechanism in the Muskoka River watershed. As such they have contributed to such important causes as log drives, flood control, water conservation, and the operation of mills and hydroelectric stations.

Undoubtedly the most famous lakes on the Muskoka River are the Muskoka Lakes: Muskoka, Rosseau and Joseph. The raw, powerful beauty of their rocky islands and peninsulas and wind-blown pines, combined with their early accessibility, made them the location of Muskoka's first resorts and cottages. Other lakes that gained early fame for their beauty and resorts include Lake of Bays and Mary, Fairy and Peninsula lakes, all surrounded by lush, rolling green hills. Today virtually all of the major lakes in the Muskoka watershed, and scores of smaller ones, are ringed by cottages and bustle with recreational activity. A few, notably in Algonquin Park, are still delightfully lost in wilderness solitude.

The two principal historical developments associated with the lakes in the Muskoka River system — steamboat navigation and the rise of resorts and tourism — are also those most extensively researched and written about. That's hardly surprising. When we recall the era of the big steamers and the golden years of some of Canada's finest resorts, we cannot help but feel those were exciting and romantic times. The thousands of cottagers and vacationers who enjoy the lakes now often have added reason to inquire into past events on these waters: many of them come from families who began vacationing in Muskoka a century ago. The history of the lakes becomes an integral part of the history of their families.

For a detailed account of the steamboating days in Muskoka I highly recommend Richard Tatley's two-volume work, *The Steamboating Era in the Muskokas*. This exhaustively researched effort, complete with scores of historical photographs, is almost comprehensive enough to be called a history of Muskoka. It deals with resorts and tourism, settlement, lumbering and other activities influenced by steamboat navigation, as well as the steamboats themselves and the people who operated them. *Muskoka's Grand Hotels*, by Barbaranne Boyer, provides an interesting look at many of the famous resort hotels that sprang up around Muskoka's lakes. In addition there are dozens of other books and articles that approach steamboating and tourism in Muskoka from various perspectives.

In the face of the existence of such an excellent selection of reference materials, I intend here to give only a brief outline of the steamboating era and the rise of resorts and tourism on the lakes of the Muskoka River system. Before we get into that, however, let's take a look at something generally overlooked in other accounts.

THE NATURAL HISTORY OF MUSKOKA'S LAKES

The staggering number of lakes in the Muskoka River watershed boast a variety of interesting and even dramatic origins — how many watersheds, for instance, have a meteorite crater?

Virtually all of the major lakes, and a large proportion of the smaller ones, owe their origins to the glaciers of the last Ice Age. They occupy basins gouged into the bedrock by the four ice sheets that overran the watershed during the last million years. The scraped, rocky shores of many of these basins give the lakes their characteristic rugged beauty.

The configuration of the basins, and hence of the lakes that filled them, depends largely on the structure and hardness of the rock. The tilted layers of gneiss that underlie the Muskoka River watershed gave rise to an erosional landscape characterized by parallel ridges and lines of hills with intervening troughs and valleys carved into the softer layers. The glaciers tended to excavate elongated basins in these valleys (that's why so many lakes lie between the parallel sweep of the ridges and hills around them). Although this is most noticeable in the western part of the watershed — the linear islands and peninsulas of Lake Joseph and western Lake Muskoka, narrow finger-like lakes such as those found along the Gibson River — it is a common trait throughout the river

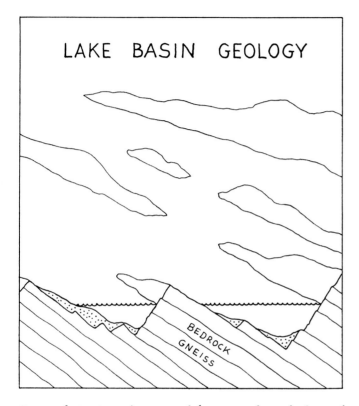

LAKE BASIN GEOLOGY

During the Ice Age, glaciers carved basins into the weaker layers of tilted bedrock gneiss that underlie the Muskoka watershed. Lakes filled many of these basins afterwards. The harder layers stand up as islands, peninsulas and of course shorelines. Most medium-sized and larger lakes occupy several interconnected basins.

system. It becomes more obvious on some lakes when you examine a depth-contour map which shows basins not apparent from the shoreline configuration.

Glacial excavation of fractured and heavily jointed rock along ancient fault lines, often running at right angles to the ridges, created the basins of several lakes, most notably Smoke Lake in the headwaters of the Oxtongue River. Fault-line basins, often manifesting themselves as narrow bays cutting across the ridges, also comprise parts of many lakes, this again being most noticeable in the areas of low relief close to Georgian Bay. Go Home Lake is a good example of this.

To gain some idea of the enormous erosive power of the ice, you need only look at the depths of some of the lakes in the Muskoka watershed. At least 12 lakes plunge to depths exceeding 50 metres (164 feet), and the northern basin of Lake Joseph is an incredible 93.9 metres (308 feet) deep. Until you know how deep they are, it's sometimes not obvious that many lakes occupy glacially-gouged basins. Often substantial sections of the shorelines are formed in sand, gravel or clay, not bounded by rock. However, these loose materials were merely deposited in and around the basins by glacial meltwaters or by rivers after the ice melted. We can thank such deposition for the many excellent sand beaches found in the Muskoka watershed.

Not all lakes of glacial origin lie in bedrock basins. A few, mainly smaller ones with modest outflows, are impounded behind natural dams of stones and silt dumped by the melting glacier. Larger outflows tend to cut fairly quickly down through this glacial till and drain the lake away.

Another type of glacially formed lake is the *kettle lake*. As the glacier melted, blocks of ice often became detached from the margin. Meltwaters would then build up layer upon layer of sand and gravel around them as a level plain or delta. When the ice blocks melted, depressions called kettles remained. If the water table was high enough, a kettle lake filled all or parts of the kettle depressions.

A good example of a kettle lake in the Muskoka River watershed is Spring Lake, on the north side of Highway 60 just east of Dwight. It lies on the delta formed over 11,000 years ago by the Oxtongue River, which at that time carried huge quantities of sand-laden meltwaters down off the Algonquin Highland.

At the same time another kettle (occupied by a small pond today) took shape on what was then the rapidly growing delta of the Big East River spillway just north of Huntsville. It's entirely possible that the blocks of ice responsible for these two kettles were icebergs that had become stranded in the shallows where the rivers entered Lake Algonquin. The elevations of both kettles coincide with the Lake Algonquin water level in those areas.

Of all the lakes in the Muskoka River watershed, no doubt Skeleton Lake boasts the most dramatic origins. Evidence strongly suggests that the main basin of Skeleton Lake, comprising just over half of the lake, is the remnant of a meteorite crater formed millions of years ago. Although considerably modified by weathering and glaciation, this crater still shows up with startling clarity on a depth-contour map as a nearly circular basin about 3.6 kilometres (2.2 miles) in diameter and over 55 metres (180 feet) deep all the way around the perimeter. The crater rim forms the north shore of Skeleton Lake along the Tomelin Bluffs.

During the 11,000 years since the recession of the ice from the Muskoka watershed, ongoing geologic processes have continued to create lakes. For instance, along streams such as the lower Big East River that have carved shifting, meandering channels across flat, sandy valley floors, we find oxbow lakes. These U-shaped ponds are actually abandoned sections of river channel that result whenever the river cuts through the neck of one of its meanders. The abandoned loop soon becomes separated from the main channel by sandbars. New oxbow lakes are still being formed today, and scores of old ones, many of them just swampy remnants, litter the flood plains of the Big East and other streams.

The Big East River has also formed several small lakes and will undoubtedly form more in the process of extending its delta out into Lake Vernon. Deltaic sands and silts have closed off what were originally bays.

The plunge pools of many waterfalls on the Muskoka River are large and deep enough to qualify as small lakes. Scooped out by the swirling currents at the base of the falls, these oval basins often contain a central sandbar that may project as an island at low water. The Bracebridge Falls pool was an important harbour during the steamboat era.

Biological processes also work to create new lakes, or ponds, to be precise. Along hundreds of creeks throughout the watershed, beavers have built countless dams to impound ponds. Altogether beaver ponds flood a substantial area and they're an integral component of stream ecosystems.

Man-made dams have created dozens of new lakes on the Muskoka River and increased the surface area and elevation of many natural ones. In most instances the new water bodies are just small ponds: mill ponds, farm ponds, fish ponds. During the latter 19th century the lumbermen built dams that impounded several much larger ponds to store water for their log drives. Notable among these are Distress Pond and Finlayson Pond on the Big East River. They still exist today.

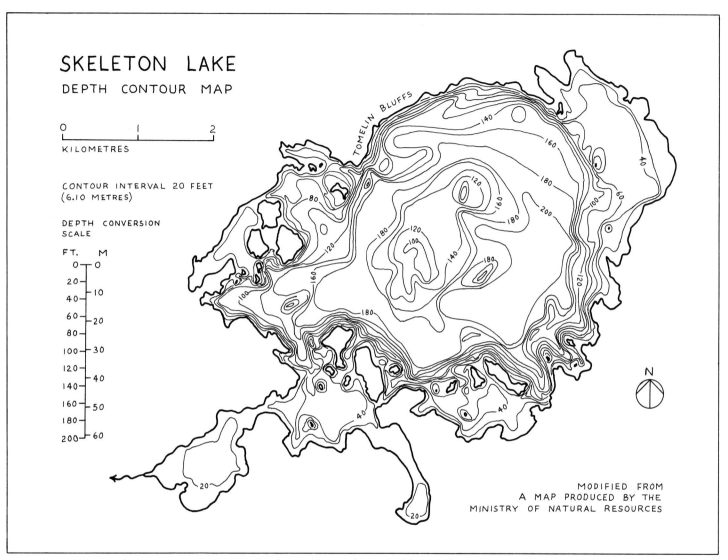

SKELETON LAKE

DEPTH CONTOUR MAP

0   1   2

KILOMETRES

CONTOUR INTERVAL 20 FEET
(6.10 METRES)

DEPTH CONVERSION
SCALE

FT.	M
0	0
20	
40	10
60	20
80	
100	30
120	40
140	
160	50
180	
200	60

TOMELIN BLUFFS

N

MODIFIED FROM
A MAP PRODUCED BY THE
MINISTRY OF NATURAL RESOURCES

The ancient meteorite crater that forms the main basin of Skeleton Lake shows up dramatically on this depth-contour map. The present configuration of the crater floor is largely a result of glacial erosion. Although very scenic, Skeleton Lake gives few obvious surface clues to its unique origins — except to geologists.

The largest artificial lakes on the Muskoka River are a result of hydroelectric development. The Big Eddy Reservoir, created in 1941 as part of the Big Eddy power development on the Musquash River, covers about 160 hectares (400 acres). The Matthiasville Reservoir on the South Muskoka is about half that size.

Despite the constant creation of new water bodies, the number of lakes in the Muskoka watershed is actually decreasing. Geological and biological processes not only form lakes, they destroy them too. Like waterfalls, lakes are just temporary features of river systems, with much shorter lifespans than the streams that feed and drain them.

On the deeper lakes geological processes act first to diminish them. Erosion of the outlet channel slowly lowers the water level while at the same time sand and silt carried in by the tributaries gradually fill the basin up. Both of these processes act very slowly on Canadian Shield rivers such as the Muskoka. The gneiss that forms the controlling sills under the outlets is extremely resistant to erosion (and of course dams built on top can delay the erosion almost indefinitely). Not only that, the water flowing over these sills is remarkably free of suspended sediment particles that could speed up the abrasion of the rock. Most sediments brought down by the tributaries settle out in the still waters of the lakes.

The filling in of lakes by sediment deposition also proceeds at a snail's pace for the most part. The streams of the Muskoka River system carry a relatively light load of eroded materials due to the extensive forest cover and bedrock in the watershed. Of the major lakes, only Lake Vernon is shrinking at a fairly rapid pace as a result of sediment deposition. That's because its principal tributary, the Big East River,

is still actively eroding its sandy valley and building a delta out into Lake Vernon at its mouth. Even so, Lake Vernon will exist for tens of thousands of years yet, and the other big lakes can expect lifespans vastly longer. Of course we'll always have beaver ponds and oxbow lakes, these being constantly created anew. The lakes of glacial origin are the ones that will disappear from the landscape.

When a lake becomes shallow enough through geological processes, or if it started out shallow, biological processes come into play and speed up the conversion to dry land. Once the depth is reduced sufficiently that plants can grow on the bottom (at which point, biologically, a lake becomes a pond) layers of organic material begin to accumulate as plants die. This further reduces depth and area, creating conditions suitable for species in the next stage of an ecological succession of plant and animal communities. These stages progress, each paving the way for the next, slightly drier one, until a stable climax community — usually a forest in Muskoka — eventually evolves.

Since the Ice Age, countless shallow lakes, bays, ponds, bogs and marshes in the Muskoka watershed have disappeared through natural ecological succession, and the process is well advanced on hundreds more. Marshes and other wetlands (many originally lakes and ponds) provide a rich habitat for a wide variety of plants and wildlife and, like lakes, act as natural water-storage reservoirs. They should not be artificially filled in or drained for industrial, commercial or residential development.

The most serious threat today to the lakes and other water bodies of the Muskoka River system, and all across the Canadian Shield, is the high acidity caused by acid precipitation. The metamorphic gneiss underlying the watershed does not contain elements that would help neutralize the acidity in the way that the limestone found further south does. Some lakes are so acidic that virtually nothing can live in them, and the rest are threatened to varying degrees. Unless both Canada and the United States quickly and effectively control the sources of acid precipitation (sulphur dioxide emissions from smelters and coal-fired generating stations are the big culprit) we face the possibility that practically all life in Muskoka's beautiful lakes will die.

And that would be a terrible tragedy indeed.

LARGEST AND DEEPEST LAKES IN THE MUSKOKA RIVER WATERSHED

Lakes with surface area over 5.0 square kilometres (excluding islands) or maximum depth exceeding 50 metres.

Lake	Area		Max. Depth		Height above sea level (summer)	
	km²	mi.²	metres	feet	metres	feet
Muskoka	120	46	67.1	220	225.3	739
Lake of Bays	68	26	79.3	260	315.2	1034
Rosseau	63	24	90.2	296	226.0	741
Joseph	53	20	93.9	308	226.0	741
Hollow	32	12.3	73.2	240	355.6	1166
Skeleton	20	7.7	64.6	212	280.7	921
Vernon	15.4	5.9	37.2	122	283.8	931
Mary	10.6	4.1	56.4	185	280.7	921
Burnt Island	9.6	3.7	32.9	108	428.5	1405
Peninsula	8.3	3.2	34.2	112	283.8	931
Three Mile	8.2	3.2	11.0	36	245.5	805*
Fairy	7.0	2.7	69.5	228	283.8	931
Ragged	6.6	2.5	37.8	124	432.3	1418
Go Home	6.6	2.5	32.6	107	185.3	608
Smoke	6.3	2.4	57.9	190	417.8	1370
McCraney	3.9	1.5	61.3	201	444.9	1459
Kimball	2.0	0.8	65.5	215	358.2	1175*
South Wildcat	1.1	0.4	57.0	187	445.1	1460*

*Elevation approximate. All other lakes regulated by government control dams.

Back in the 1820s and 1830s explorers examined the Muskoka River to determine if it might serve as a connecting link in a proposed canal between Georgian Bay and the Ottawa River. They found the river quite unsuited for that purpose. The great descent, numerous waterfalls and the hard, unyielding rock of the Shield would have made the construction of the necessary locks and by-pass canals a difficult and prohibitively expensive proposition. Although the Muskoka River provided an excellent canoe route of great benefit to the Indians, fur traders, trappers and explorers — and today for canoe trippers — it would never become a navigable route like the Rideau or Trent-Severn waterways.

Within the Muskoka River system, however, the huge lakes and lake chains provided admirable opportunities for inland navigation (a fact noted by canal explorer Alexander Shirreff in 1829). It was inevitable that these lakes would become an integral part of the local transportation network after settlement in the watershed began in 1859. Early roads in Muskoka were little more than rough trails winding through the hills, when they existed at all. The first settlers, surveyors and lumbermen used the lakes and rivers for travel whenever possible. Canoes, rafts, rowboats, the occasional sailboat and even a bizarre horse-powered craft were pressed into service. And before long, someone decided to take advantage of the true navigation potential of the big inland lakes.

That someone was Alexander Peter Cockburn, an ambitious young man from Kirkfield, Ontario. As a result of explorations in the fall of 1865 that took him across most of the major lakes in the Muskoka watershed, he became con-

vinced that the settlement and lumbering potential of the district gave it a bright future. He proposed to the government that he'd put a steamboat on the Muskoka Lakes if they, in return, would bring in policies to encourage more settlement and undertake some navigation improvements, notably a lock to by-pass some minor rapids on the Indian River between lakes Muskoka and Rosseau.

Evidently encouraged by the response he got, Cockburn forged ahead with his steamship plans. A few months later, in the late spring of 1866, he launched the sidewheeler *Wenonah* on Lake Muskoka near Gravenhurst. She began carrying passengers and freight to points around Lake Muskoka and up the Muskoka River to Bracebridge, and soon started towing booms of logs as well. The immense practical benefits of the steamer to the Muskoka frontier were immediately apparent.

Partly as a result of Cockburn's lobbying efforts, the Ontario government passed the Free Grant and Homesteads Act in 1868. This significantly increased the numbers of settlers moving to Muskoka and assured the financial success of the *Wenonah*. In 1869, also due in part to pressure from Cockburn, as well as from settlers around the lakes, work finally began on a government navigation lock on the Indian River at Port Carling. That year too Cockburn placed the small steamer *Waubamik* on Lake Rosseau. Not until the completion of the lock in 1871, however, could boats navigate between lakes Rosseau and Muskoka.

In 1870 excavation began of a very short canal through the narrow isthmus that separates lakes Rosseau and Joseph at Port Sandfield. Government engineers decided that was an easier way to join the lakes for navigation purposes than removing rock obstructions in the natural connecting link,

THE "NIPISSING". *This attractive side-wheeler, launched by A.P. Cockburn in 1887, plied the Muskoka Lakes until 1914. The Segwun was built on her hull in 1925. Cockburn's original Nipissing had burned in 1886, fifteen years after it first began service.* · Archives of Ontario Acc. 9912-1-40

the Joseph River (although that was done later). The Port Carling Lock and the Port Sandfield Cut, along with some other minor channel improvements, opened up the entire Muskoka Lakes to unimpeded steamboat navigation. On these famous lakes Cockburn built up what would become the largest and most successful inland steamship navigation company in Canada. It operated under a variety of names over the years but was commonly referred to locally as simply the Navigation Company.

By the latter 19th century the Muskoka Lakes were crawling with commercial steamboat traffic, feeding the economy of the surrounding district. Big passenger steamers ferried settlers, freight and mail to far-flung villages and, until 1886, to colonization roads leading to frontiers further north. Increasingly, they also carried vacationers to new resorts springing up around the rugged shores. Tugboats towed enormous booms of logs to dozens of sawmills and heavily laden scows of hemlock bark to the tanneries at Bracebridge. Supply boats carried goods to scattered farms, resorts and cottages. And soon the wealthy city folks who used the lakes as their summer playground began to cruise the waters in private steam yachts.

As settlement spread northward and eastward in the Muskoka watershed, the big lakes on the North Muskoka River and Lake of Bays on the South Muskoka became home to fleets of steamers similar in variety, though not in number, to those on the Muskoka Lakes. Apparently recognizing the benefits of Cockburn's first steamers on the Muskoka Lakes, the Ontario government sought to encourage navigation in northern Muskoka by letting a contract in 1873 for the construction of a lock and canal to circumvent a set of rapids on the North Muskoka River between Mary and Fairy lakes.

LOCKING THROUGH AT PORT CARLING, 1908.
Upstream-bound on the Indian River, the Sagamo rises to the level of the upper river as water fills the lock chamber. The "Big Chief" was flagship of the Navigation Company steamer fleet on the Muskoka Lakes for half a century.   · Archives of Ontario Acc. 2203·S·3627a

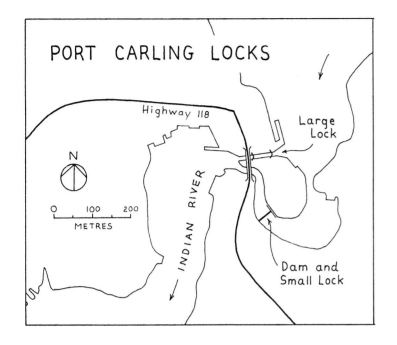

PORT CARLING LOCKS

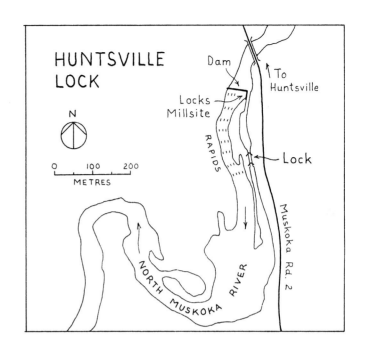

HUNTSVILLE LOCK

NAVIGATION LOCKS on the Indian River (Port Carling) and North Muskoka River (near Huntsville) formed vital links in the Muskoka transportation system during the first several decades of the steamboat era. Today pleasure boats account for practically all of the more than 20,000 lockages each season at Port Carling, and the 2,000 or so at Huntsville.

Back in 1837 explorer David Thompson first mentioned the idea of a lock at what would become Port Carling. He noted that one could be built across a neck of land to by-pass two sets of minor rapids on a loop of the Indian River. The Ontario Department of Public Works chose exactly that site when it had the original large lock constructed in 1869-71. The lock occupies a short canal excavated in bedrock. A control dam and channel improvements largely eliminated the rapids on the natural river course and made possible the small lock (1921) to serve growing small motorboat traffic.

The Port Carling Locks normally raise or lower boats scarcely .7 metres (27 inches). Rebuilt and improved at various times, they're both fully mechanized now. The Ministry of Natural Resources owns and operates these facilities. Parkland and the Port Carling pioneer museum occupy the little island between the locks.

The Huntsville Lock and its approach channels by-pass a dam and rapids on the North Muskoka River, overcoming the three-metre (10-foot) elevation difference between Mary and Fairy lakes. Constructed originally of timber for the Department of Public Works in 1873-75, and later faced with concrete, the all-manual lock was completely rebuilt in 1987-89 by the Ministry of Natural Resources. An attractive park surrounds the lock site.

HUNTSVILLE LOCK, *about 1907. The Huntsville Navigation Company's ornate Dortha, bound for Port Sydney from Huntsville, waits to be lowered. Note the wood construction of the lock, and the manual gates, operated by pushing on the projecting beams.* · Archives of Ontario Acc. 13889-2

With some associated channel improvements, completed in 1877, this opened up a navigable waterway stretching all the way from Port Sydney up through Huntsville and on to Port Vernon (Hoodstown) at the west end of Lake Vernon.

The steamer *Northern*, launched at Port Sydney in June 1877, was the first to ply the new northern route. Captain Alfred Denton emerged as the principal figure in this opera-tion. He expanded his fleet as settlement and industry increased in the townships around the northern lakes. By 1888 he could run steamers into Peninsula Lake via a 1.2-kilometre (.7-mile) government canal dredged along the marshy creek that originally joined it to Fairy Lake. At the east end of Peninsula Lake a stagecoach and wagon service operated over a narrow height of land to connect with steamers on Lake of Bays.

Steamboat service on Lake of Bays began in 1878, when Joseph Huckins had A.P. Cockburn's *Waubamik* transported overland from Bracebridge to Baysville and relaunched as the *Dean*. Lake of Bays provided a large sheet of navigable water with virtually no improvements required. From the stand-point of navigation, access and development, Lake of Bays and the big lakes on the North Muskoka became part of an integrated hinterland served out of Huntsville by a navigation company exceeded only by the one founded by Cockburn on the Muskoka Lakes (of course, as on the Muskoka Lakes, lumber companies and other firms and individuals owned a number of tugs, supply boats and small passenger steamers in addition to those belonging to the big navigation companies).

The Huntsville Navigation Company was originally built up by George Marsh. Marsh first entered the navigation business on Lake of Bays in 1884, when he launched the *Mary Louise* to compete with steamers owned by Joseph Huckins. Later he expanded his operations to the North Muskoka River lakes where Alfred Denton already operated. By 1895 he had pur-chased Denton's interests and his firm had emerged as the principal navigation company on Lake of Bays and the North Muskoka lakes.

George Marsh was instrumental in spearheading the con-struction of the Portage Railway to replace the old stagecoach and wagon service between Peninsula Lake and Lake of Bays. This unique little railway, which operated from 1904 to 1959, was a considerable impetus to early economic development on Lake of Bays and to the fortunes of the Huntsville Naviga-tion Company. Niall MacKay's *By Steam Boat and Steam Train* provides an informative account, complemented by numer-ous photographs, of the Portage Railway and the steamers that connected with it.

You need only look at a map of Muskoka to appreciate the extent to which the steamers operating on the big lakes of the Muskoka River system could influence settlement and economic development in the district. The Muskoka Lakes, Lake of Bays and the four-lake chain on the North Muskoka collectively cover 345 square kilometres (133 square miles), their numerous arms and bays poke into some 20 townships. Few of the settled parts of Muskoka are more than a few kilometres from them; all of the major towns and many of the smaller villages grew on their shores or on navigable riv-ers connected to them. And the big resort hotels that had made Muskoka famous by the end of the 19th century all overlooked the panoramic expanses of these same lakes.

When Muskoka was first opened for settlement, resorts and tourism were far from the minds of government offi-cials, surveyors and the early pioneers trickling in to begin a new life on the frontier. They saw farmland (or what they optimistically thought was farmland), water power for mills, pine timber, and to a lesser extent fur-bearing animals. They also saw, and no doubt appreciated, the tremendous beauty of the lakes and the opportunities for fishing and sightseeing, but many of them would have laughed at the notion that people might want to trek up into this remote, untamed country for a vacation.

Nonetheless, handfuls of tourists journeyed up to the lakes virtually on the heels of the first settlers in 1860. Attracted north by a sense of adventure and stories of the great scenery and fishing, they paddled on the lakes and streams, camped on the islands and peninsulas. Within a couple of decades some of them established the first summer cottages on their favourite campsites. Less ambitious tourists stayed at hotels or inns in fledgling villages like Gravenhurst and Bracebridge, or boarded with farmers near the lakes.

The organized summer resort and tourism industry in the Muskoka watershed got its real start in 1869. That year a New York entrepreneur named William H. Pratt visited the Muskoka Lakes and came away so impressed by the beauty and character of these remote northern waters that he decided to build a large resort hotel at the head of Lake Rosseau. Rosseau House (or Pratt's, as it was often called) opened in 1871 at the site of Rosseau village and thrived despite its high rates and isolated location. It proved especially popular with wealthy Americans; so too did Summit House, built soon afterwards at the head of Lake Joseph by Brampton lawyer Hamilton Fraser (the character and aesthetics of the two upper lakes was often considered superior to that of Lake Muskoka at the time).

These resorts, and others that followed, depended on A.P. Cockburn's steamers to transport guests up the lakes from Gravenhurst. Indeed, had it not been for the steamers it's unlikely resorts would have been established on the Muskoka Lakes at such an early date. Cockburn quickly recognized the potential importance of the resort and tourism trade for his steamer operations and the local economy. Along with the resort owners he began actively publicizing Muskoka's natural advantages in an effort to attract vacationers.

The existence of the steamers and the beauty of the lakes notwithstanding, it was the arrival of the railway that gave a major boost to the resort industry on Muskoka's lakes. Up until then everyone journeying to Muskoka, rowdy lumberjacks and rich Americans alike, had to suffer the bone-jarring stagecoach ride from Washago to Gravenhurst along the infamous Muskoka Road. But when the Northern Railway was extended to Lake Muskoka at Gravenhurst in 1875, vacationers could travel in relative comfort all the way up from Toronto and beyond, board the steamers and proceed up the lakes to the resort hotels. The railway company added its advertising resources to the growing cause of promoting Muskoka as a vacationers' and sportsmen's paradise. As Muskoka became more famous in the coming years, dozens of newspaper articles, guidebooks and brochures lavishly described and praised the scenic beauty of its lakes, waterfalls and rivers.

During the 1880s more resorts began to appear around the Muskoka Lakes, and the trend accelerated in the 1890s. Some had originally started in a small way years before, when settlers with land bordering the lakes took in occasional sportsmen for lodgings. When these settlers realized they could make money this way — probably more than they could trying to farm on bedrock — they gradually expanded

THE CANAL. Linking Fairy and Peninsula lakes, it's the longest artificial waterway in the Muskoka River system. The Ontario Department of Public Works dug it in 1886-88 along a swampy creek valley. In this photograph the Huntsville Navigation Company's flagship, the Algonquin (original version, 1906 to 1927), steams past the Sarona.

· Archives of Ontario Acc. 13889-14b

FERNDALE, *Lake Rosseau. This was just one of many resort hotels that sprang up on the Muskoka Lakes in the late 1800s and early 1900s to serve wealthy vacationers who found Muskoka a fashionable as well as scenic destination.* · Archives of Ontario Acc. 9939-20

and improved their guest facilities. Other establishments rose practically overnight as imposing hotels set amongst the pines, high above the rocky shorelines.

Although the resorts ranged from the lavish to the spartan, Muskoka quickly gained a wide reputation for its luxury hotels in which guests could relax in the quiet, dignified comfort consistent with upper-class life at the end of the 19th century. These naturally catered to the wealthy, Americans especially, but to more and more Canadians too as time went on. By 1909, 76 resorts on the Muskoka Lakes offered accommodations for nearly 5,000 guests. It may not have been an exaggeration to say that the Muskoka Lakes had become the summer resort capital of Ontario.

The first private cottages on the Muskoka Lakes date back to the late 1870s and early 1880s. Although families of comparatively modest means did erect simple, unpretentious structures, the big story in the late 19th and early 20th centuries was the activities of the rich. Wealthy families quickly purchased islands and other choice real estate on the lakes and built huge mansions to use for their summer vacations. A section of shoreline near Beaumaris on Lake Muskoka has become known as Millionaires' Row.

The development of the resort and tourism industry on Lake of Bays and the North Muskoka River lakes lagged somewhat behind the Muskoka Lakes. That was largely because steamboats and rail access came a few years later to these more remote waters. The railway, for instance, didn't reach Huntsville until 1886. However, in the late 1890s resorts started to multiply around Mary, Fairy and Peninsula lakes and Lake of Bays. One of the earliest was Deerhurst Inn, founded in 1896 on Peninsula Lake. Vacationers took the trains to Huntsville, where they boarded steamers serving the resorts and communities around the lakes.

Interestingly, the opening of another railroad in the late 1800s led to the establishment of some early resorts on lakes in an unlikely part of the Muskoka River system. By the First World War a handful of hotels and wilderness lodges had been built in the headwaters of the Oxtongue River in Algonquin Park, on Smoke, Canoe, Joe and Burnt Island lakes. Vacationers reached this remote area along a railway constructed through the Park in the 1890s by lumber baron J.R. Booth. No passenger steamers operated on the lakes. Guests travelled by canoe or stagecoach to the lodges most distant from the railway line. Rail access also resulted in the establishment of boys' and girls' camps and cottages in the same area. None of the old resorts survive; only the Arowhon Pines lodge, built in the 1930s, carries on now.

The period from the mid-1890s up until the First World War might be considered the heydey of Muskoka's lavish upper-class resort hotels, and of the big passenger steamers which by that time catered largely to the resort trade. That era saw the opening of the Royal Muskoka Hotel on lake Rosseau (it was reputed to be one of the finest in Canada), the commencement of work on the equally sumptuous Bigwin Inn on Lake of Bays, and the launching in 1906 of the largest of the Muskoka Lakes steamboats, the *Sagamo*. Several other big steamers made their debut during those comfortable times as well.

The nature of navigation and tourism on the lakes of the Muskoka River system has changed immensely since the early years of the 20th century. Once vital arteries of commerce and transport, the lakes today primarily serve the recreational boater. And while scores of resorts, ranging from four-star hotels to modest rental cabins, still thrive, and the wealthy continue to maintain their waterfront mansions, the private cottage now dominates the tourism scene. The elegant old resorts that catered to the upper classes 80 years ago have closed, burned down or evolved into modern facilities that reflect today's active lifestyles and a society in which middle-class values have become entrenched.

The expansion and improvement of the road network in Muskoka, and the age of the automobile, contributed most to the demise of the waterways as important transportation routes and helped propel the steamers to near extinction. It became easier and more convenient to drive to resorts, cottages and villages around the lakes, to bring supplies in by truck. The increasing popularity of private gas-powered motorboats also took business away from the passenger and supply steamers. Motorboats first appeared on the lakes in the early 1900s; today literally thousands of them scoot about. For many years prior to the age of mass-produced fibreglass models, the Muskoka Lakes supported a thriving boatbuilding industry noted especially for its sleek mahogany launches.

The once bustling steam tug business on the lakes ended as a result of changes in the resource-based industries that supported it. A decline in lumbering meant fewer booms of logs to be towed to the mills, and of course when lumber companies started using trucks rather than the rivers and lakes to transport their logs, tugs were not required at all. The tugs that hauled scows of hemlock bark from all around the lakes to the tanneries at Bracebridge and Huntsville became redundant when the local supply of bark dwindled and the tanneries closed or began using chemicals rather than bark in the leather-tanning process — this all by the 1930s.

After the 1920s the big passenger steamboats served primarily as cruise boats (they also carried mail, an important source of revenue, and declining amounts of freight). Except during the Depression they remained fairly viable ventures until the late 1940s. The 100 Mile Cruise on the Muskoka Lakes, anchored by the flagship *Sagamo*, gained renown throughout eastern Canada and the northeastern United States after it was inaugurated in the 1920s.

After the Second World War fewer and fewer people patronized the steamboats, preferring more active forms of recreation centred on their cottages and motorboats. In 1948 the last steamer on Lake of Bays, the *Iroquois*, ceased operations; in 1952 the *Algonquin* carried its last passengers between Huntsville and the Portage Railway. Stringent new safety regulations that required expensive alterations dealt a serious blow to the Muskoka Lakes fleet, and the loss of the mail contract later added to their financial woes. The *Sagamo* and the *Segwun* limped on until 1958 and then pulled into the Muskoka Wharf at Gravenhurst apparently never to sail again. After 92 years the steamboat era in Muskoka had come to an end.

Or had it really? Of course everyone in the district knows now about the successful restoration of the *Segwun* and its return to active cruise-boat service in 1981. The oldest operating steamboat in North America (it was originally launched as the *Nipissing* in 1887) the *Segwun* has quickly become one of Muskoka's prime summer attractions.

Although the numbers of cottages increased steadily through earlier decades, the tremendous growth in the cottage industry on the lakes of the Muskoka watershed has largely been a post-Second World War phenomenon. Muskoka's proximity and good road connections to the cities of the south, and a prosperous middle-class with plenty of leisure time, fuelled this explosion of waterfront development. Cottages burgeoned around the major lakes, where tourism had first begun, then soon started springing up around dozens of smaller ones and along the North and South branches of the Muskoka River. Somewhere in the neighbourhood of 20,000 cottages now exist in the Muskoka River watershed. With many of the shorelines as densely populated as a city street, the challenge of the future lies in controlling waterfront development to preserve the natural beauty of the lakes and streams, protect water quality, and improve opportunities for public access.

Who would have thought, little more than a century and a quarter ago, that the wild and remote lakelands of the Muskoka River system would become the heart of that bustling belt along the fringe of the Canadian Shield known in the south today as "Cottage Country."

CHAPTER 11

Lumbermen's Highway: The Log-Driving Era on the Muskoka River

Springtime. Imagine the river swollen by meltwaters, swirling past dark cedars and pine and the gaunt skeletons of leafless maple and birch. Imagine the river filled to the brim not only with racing icy waters, but with thousands of pine logs bumping and churning in the current, piling through narrow rock chutes or catapulting over thundering falls. And imagine, too, the river drivers, those hardy lumbermen trailing the mass of logs in their pointer boats, leaping skillfully from log to log with their peaveys and pike-poles, levering and prodding the timber away from back eddies or snags, or wading waist deep in the frigid waters to free the beginnings of a jam before it can grow into a quivering monster that completely blocks the river.

You don't see scenes like these anymore on the Muskoka River. The log-driving era, one of the most colourful and exciting chapters in the story of the river, is now just history. It's been over 40 years since any logs came down the Muskoka, but for more than eight decades the annual log drive was a familiar event, a dramatic reminder of the once dominant role of the lumber industry in the economy of the region.

When lumbermen first began to stalk the virgin forests of eastern Canada they naturally turned to the rivers to transport their logs down to the sawmills or to ports for export. Teams of horses or oxen could draw logs only a few kilome-

tres; bulldozers to carve roads deep into the wilderness and trucks to haul logs out along them were inventions still centuries into the future; and railways, which in any case didn't become prevalent in Canada until the 1850s, could not feasibly be extended into the heart of all cutting areas. Thus the waterways provided the only practical alternative for moving large quantities of timber long distances. By 1880 lumber companies were driving logs down 234 rivers in eastern Canada.

In the 1930s trucks began rapidly replacing rivers as the means of moving logs. The switch from water to road transport was virtually complete in many watersheds, including the Muskoka, by the end of the Second World War. Log drives still continue today on a number of rivers where it is still cheaper and more convenient to transport the logs that way.

Lumbering and log drives in what is now eastern Canada began in the early 1600s, soon after the French colonists arrived. Although limited exports took place, most of the timber was for local use and the logs were sawn in water-powered mills. Not until the early 1800s, nearly half a century after the British conquest, did Canadian lumbering really begin to boom and to supply an export market.

Up until 1808 Britain obtained most of its timber from the Baltic area of Europe. But that year France (with whom Britain was at war at the time) instigated a successful blockade that largely cut off the Baltic supply. In order to secure timber needed for shipbuilding and construction, Britain turned to North America on an unprecedented scale. Canadian lumbering rapidly expanded. Even when Baltic supplies became available again, Britain instituted preferential tariffs that favoured the new North American supply.

The British trade in those days was primarily in square timber. Only the finest-quality pine was acceptable. Skilled axe-wielding lumberjacks squared the logs in the bush — a practice that wasted up to half of the wood but allowed the logs to be stowed more compactly in the ships. On small and medium-sized rivers the squared logs floated down individually; on major streams, like the Ottawa and St. Lawrence rivers, they were formed into rafts for the rest of the journey to the ships waiting at Quebec City.

Logging and log drives in the Muskoka River watershed were still nearly half a century into the future when the British square timber trade took off. Since the domestic market for lumber was largely concentrated in the East, and Quebec City was the port for overseas shipment from the St. Lawrence River basin, the lumbermen naturally tackled first the watersheds of the closest rivers, the direct tributaries of the St. Lawrence and Ottawa. The Muskoka River flowed the wrong way, westward into Georgian Bay (its waters do eventually reach the St. Lawrence by a roundabout route through the Great Lakes).

As the supply of quality pine in the eastern watersheds declined, the lumbermen pushed further west, commencing operations along rivers flowing into western Lake Ontario, then Lake Erie and soon Lake Huron. A growing American market for Canadian wood — sawlogs, boards and planks

rather than square timber — also helped fuel this westward expansion. Timber reserves in the eastern United States were nearing depletion and at the same time settlement was expanding out onto the treeless prairies of the Midwest. By the 1860s the American market for Canadian timber would exceed the British requirements.

In the early 1850s the lumbermen began to set their sights on the virgin forests of the rivers flowing into Georgian Bay. Logs and lumber from this area could be conveniently shipped by water to Chicago and other American centres on lakes Michigan and Huron, and after 1855 by rail from Collingwood to eastern markets.

The first logging operations in the Muskoka River watershed began in late 1853. That's when William Hamilton of Penetanguishene built his water-powered sawmill at Three Rock Chute near the mouth of the Musquash and began to cut pine in the vicinity. No doubt some of this timber was floated downriver to the mill — the first log drives in the Muskoka watershed.

The main thrust of logging on the Muskoka began in 1856. That year the government of Canada issued a number of timber licences along the Moon and Musquash rivers.

In the mid-1850s virgin wilderness covered all of the Muskoka River watershed. Settlement wouldn't begin until the end of the decade; no roads yet led into this lake-strewn hinterland with its seemingly inexhaustible reserves of pine (the only species of interest to the big lumber companies during that era). Thus it is hardly surprising that lumbering began on the lower reaches of the river closest to Georgian Bay. That was the most convenient area to bring in men and supplies, and to float the logs out from.

As time went by, logging operations expanded further

upstream. By 1860 men and supplies could be brought into Lake Muskoka along the new Muskoka Road, and by the following year the lumber companies, Canadian and American firms, were cutting around the shores of Lake Muskoka and the lower reaches of the North and South Muskoka rivers. Since it wasn't practical to ship logs out of the watershed along the Muskoka Road, the companies drove all the timber down the Musquash and Moon rivers (most went down the Musquash) to Georgian Bay. There they gathered it into booms and had it towed to Georgian Bay sawmilling centres such as Collingwood and Owen Sound, or even across Lake Huron to American centres. Some of the logs were sawn in the Muskoka Mills right at the mouth of the Musquash. Square timber for the British market was shipped east to Quebec.

By the early 1870s logging operations had spread well up into the Lake Rosseau · Lake Joseph area and the Lake of Bays and Huntsville districts. Lumber companies drove logs all the way from Lake Vernon and Lake of Bays to Georgian Bay, a distance of 120 kilometres (75 miles). Although that wasn't an excessive distance by Canadian log-driving standards, the numerous waterfalls and large lakes along the route made it an arduous and time-consuming task. By that time a large proportion of the cut was in the form of sawlogs. The square timber trade, strong in the 1850s, was quickly dying out.

The year 1875 stands out as an important one in the history of Muskoka River lumbering. Up until then logging operations hadn't reached their full potential because of the long and difficult drives required to get the logs out of the district. The market for lumber within Muskoka was still quite limited and water-powered sawmills required only a small quantity of logs, relatively speaking, to meet local needs.

However, in 1875, partly due to the efforts of the big lumber companies, the Northern Railway was extended into the Muskoka watershed, terminating then at Gravenhurst on Lake Muskoka. For the first time it became practical to establish a large sawmilling industry right in the Muskoka watershed; the lumber could be shipped out to market by rail. No longer did the companies logging upstream from Lake Muskoka have to drive all the way to Georgian Bay. They built big steam-powered sawmills on the shores of Lake Muskoka near Gravenhurst — so many, in fact, that by the 1880s the village was often referred to as Sawdust City and had become one of the leading sawmill centres on the Canadian Shield. When the railway opened north through Bracebridge and Huntsville in 1886, large sawmill operations grew in those communities as well.

After 1875 logging rapidly expanded eastward up the Muskoka River system. Steam tugs soon became available on Lake of Bays and the big lakes of the North Muskoka to tow booms of logs across, and for the first time the government, the lumber companies and a private river-improvement company began to make extensive improvements on the rivers to aid the drives. By the 1890s the lumbermen had marched up into the last remaining virgin forests in the watershed, up in the headwaters of the Oxtongue, Hollow and Big East rivers on the Algonquin Highland.

Most of the logs from the Hollow and Oxtongue went down through Lake of Bays and the South Muskoka River to mills at Bracebridge and Gravenhurst, a distance of as much as 170 kilometres (105 miles). It's possible that more timber went down the South Muskoka than any other stream in the

Muskoka River system. In 1891 alone the quantity was 23 million feet. Logs from the Big East River (and also the Buck) only went as far as Huntsville after the railway began service there in 1886 and big mills were established; subsequently the North Muskoka downstream was used much less for driving logs.

Some of the log drives from the Big East and Oxtongue River headwaters ended after Ottawa Valley lumber magnate J.R. Booth built the Ottawa, Arnprior & Parry Sound Railway across the Algonquin Highland. Opened in 1897, this line passed through parts of both the Oxtongue and Big East headwaters and allowed lumber companies to establish mills up there, or ship the logs out by rail rather than driving the logs down the rivers. Some of the Huntsville-based companies built new mills on the Highland. Two of the biggest names in Muskoka River logging, however, decided it was still cheaper to continue log drives off the Highland. These were the Mickle Dyment Company (with mills at Gravenhurst) and the J.D. Shier Lumber Company of Bracebridge. Both firms logged extensively in the Hollow and Oxtongue watersheds; their logs eventually passed through Lake of Bays and down the South Muskoka.

The most fascinating log drive ever to come off the Algonquin Highland was one started in 1895 by the Gilmour Company. This Trenton-based lumber firm was the first to begin logging in the Oxtongue headwaters, in 1893. Since J.R. Booth's railway hadn't yet been built, the Gilmours had to drive their logs 445 kilometres (276 miles) to their mills at Trenton on Lake Ontario. To do so they used three different river systems — the Oxtongue (Muskoka), the Black (Severn) and the Gull-Trent — and an ingenious arrangement of diversion dams, jackladders and log slide near Dorset to move the logs over the heights of land between them. It took two years to get the logs to Trenton by this route, so in 1897, after J.R. Booth's railway opened, the Gilmours opened a new mill on Canoe Lake in the Oxtongue headwaters.

Lumbering and log drives in the Muskoka River system reached their zenith in the late 1890s. By then logging operations had encompassed the entire watershed. But the reserves of pine that fuelled the industry, that just 40 years earlier had seemed inexhaustible, were nearly depleted. The lumber companies had taken the timber with no thought to the future, no adherence to sustained-yield cutting practices. After about 1900 the lumbering industry in Muskoka rapidly declined. Never again would it so completely dominate the local economy.

Lumbering didn't die out in the Muskoka watershed. Smaller quantities of pine, other softwoods, and especially the hardwoods would sustain the industry at a more modest level of activity consistent with sound forest management. Today it still provides a livelihood, directly or indirectly, for hundreds of people in Muskoka.

With the decline of lumbering in the watershed, log drives naturally declined too. The switch to hardwoods put the drives further in jeopardy: unless peeled and allowed to dry somewhat, hardwood logs tended to sink. One firm in particular, however, perfected and extensively used hardwood driving techniques. This was Huntsville-based Muskoka Wood Manufacturing, established in 1902. Right up until 1936 this successful company conducted large drives on an annual basis down the Big East and Buck rivers, and continued to tow logs on the Huntsville Lakes until 1945.

Overall, though, log drives became less frequent and smaller through the 1920s and 1930s, and by the Second

World War had for all intents and purposes ended in the Muskoka watershed. It had become easier and less expensive to transport the logs from the bush to the mills by truck.

And so, after more than 80 years, the Muskoka River outlived its usefulness as the highway of the lumber industry. We must remember, however, that had it not been for the river, lumbering never would have risen to prominence in Muskoka at the critical time it did, a time when agriculture was faltering and the settlers desperately needed another industry to sustain them until resorts and tourism became firmly established.

THE WATER HIGHWAY

The lumbermen used the Muskoka and other rivers on the Canadian Shield to transport their logs not because these waterways provided ideal highways, but because no feasible alternative usually existed. In reality the Shield rivers — and the Muskoka was certainly no exception — posed formidable problems for the log drives. Efforts made to overcome these problems resulted in some unique inventions, impressive engineering works and, in some cases, changes to the character and scenery of the waterways that are still evident to this day.

Waterfalls and rapids represented one of the most serious log-driving obstacles. The shoals and rocky constrictions at these interruptions often precipitated logjams which, if not broken quickly, could grow to mammoth proportions and block the river for days or even weeks. At the worst waterfalls the logs would literally smash to pieces as they crashed down over the jagged rocks. It was estimated that as much as a fifth of the drive was destroyed or damaged at treacherous

South Falls, for instance. This added to already considerable losses due to logs merely absorbing water and sinking in the lakes and streams.

Lakes also seriously hindered the log drives. Except on the narrowest ones, the current could not be counted upon to carry the logs across to the outlet. The only alternative was to gather the logs into booms, warp or tow them across by one means or another, then feed them into the outlet. This cost money and slowed the drive down — especially when the process had to be repeated over and over on the lake-abundant Shield rivers.

If rapids, waterfalls and lakes didn't cause enough headaches, the log drivers were at the mercy of the flow of water in the streams. Insufficient water rendered the smaller or shallower creeks and rivers impossible to drive, and increased the possibility of jams on the larger ones. On the other hand, too much water caused streams to overflow their banks and the logs would get tangled in the adjacent bush and swamps. Or sometimes initially adequate flows declined before the drive was out, stranding the logs along the shores or in the shallows.

All of these woes affected the log drives on the Muskoka River, and by various means they were all overcome to a greater or lesser degree. During the first two decades of lumbering in the watershed, lumber companies actually made few significant improvements to aid the drives, certainly not on the main rivers utilized by many companies. Not until the 1880s did legislation allow any company undertaking improvements to collect a toll from other firms benefiting from the work. Thus in the 1870s many lumber firms in Muskoka wanted the Ontario government to undertake major improvements, notably log slides to by-pass waterfalls.

The government had built slides on some other river systems.

In the latter 1870s — no doubt in part due to pressure from the lumber companies — the Ontario government did indeed begin making improvements to the major Muskoka waterways. The work was done by the Department of Public Works. In the early 1880s a private firm, the Muskoka Slide, Dam and Boom Company, was formed to carry out and maintain log-driving improvements. It largely took over from the Department of Public Works on the Muskoka River. Its sphere of operations included the Musquash, North and South Muskoka and Buck rivers. Lumber companies paid a toll for the use of the private facilities, in proportion to the number of logs each sent down the river. Later on, the Muskoka River Improvement Company evolved, conducting drives between Hollow Lake and Lake Muskoka.

On the Big East River several Huntsville-based lumber companies jointly formed the Big East River Improvement Company, which provided log-driving aids and services until the 1920s. Individual lumber companies also undertook extensive improvements from the 1880s onwards, especially on smaller streams and in the headwaters, where smaller quantities of logs were involved.

The most important tool in the log-driving improvement arsenal was the lumbering dam. Hundreds of these wooden structures were built in the Muskoka watershed. Many of these merely drowned out difficult shoals or diverted water and logs into slides that by-passed waterfalls. Many more, however, served another extremely vital function, water storage. By significantly raising the levels of dozens of natural lakes and even creating entirely new ones (such as Distress Pond and Finlayson Pond on the Big East) these dams held

TEA LAKE DAM, Oxtongue River, in the 1920s. The Gilmour Lumber Company originally built the dam in 1893 to store water for log drives. A concrete government dam now stands on this site to regulate Tea, Smoke and Canoe lakes for recreation and flood control.   · Algonquin Park Museum #85 · Stringer

back large quantities of water that could be released when needed to flush logs down the stream channels below.

Control of water flows was particularly important on the smaller streams. To avoid having to haul logs overland any further than absolutely necessary, lumber companies pressed some remarkably small creeks into service to carry logs out to the main rivers — creeks you could easily jump across in the summer. Although the drives normally began in the spring, when water was abundant, storage dams often saved the day when the freshet proved inadequate or declined before all the logs were out. Otherwise, as the old tale goes, the men had to wring the sweat out of their shirts to raise the water level! Even on the larger rivers, bursts of water from dams could alleviate problems in shallow reaches or at rapids and falls when natural stream flows fell too low. Typically, dams might be opened for a few hours during the day, then closed to allow the water levels in the lakes or ponds behind them to recover overnight.

Most of the old lumbering dams built in the Muskoka watershed have long since washed or rotted away. If you know where to look, however, you'll still find some remains of timbers and piles of stones — and lots of rusty square spikes — that once formed their crib structure. On important lakes, government control dams replaced the lumbering dams as the log-driving era wound down, or in the years afterwards. The artificially high water levels and characteristically drowned shorelines of these lakes today (especially in the Big East, Oxtongue and Hollow River basins) are lasting vestiges of the log-driving era.

Although the numerous lakes on the Muskoka River benefited the log drivers by providing convenient water-storage reservoirs, they still represented serious obstacles that had to be crossed. In the early years of lumbering in the watershed only slow, primitive means of hauling booms of logs across the lakes existed. Lumbermen mounted a capstan (winch) on a raft and fixed the raft to a log boom. By walking around in circles and pushing bars projecting from the capstan, they laboriously winched the whole affair forward to an anchor previously dropped up ahead. This arduous process had to be repeated over and over until the lake outlet was reached. Since progress amounted at best to only 300 metres (1,000 feet) per hour, you can imagine how long it would take to cross a large lake. When circumstances permitted, the lumbermen built larger rafts and used horses to turn the capstan.

With the dawn of the steamboat era on the Muskoka Lakes, Lake of Bays and the four big lakes on the North Muskoka, steam tugs became available to speed up the task of moving booms of logs across these large water bodies (a pair of tugs operated for many years on Hollow Lake as well). Then, in 1889, a unique Ontario invention revolutionized the movement of logs down the numerous and often remote lakes of Canadian Shield rivers. This was the powerful steam Alligator, a flat-bottomed side-wheeler that could not only travel on water, but also winch itself overland between lakes on logs laid along the portage to act as rollers. An Alligator could pull a boom containing as many as 60,000 logs.

The Alligator didn't actually tow large log booms, but like the old capstan rafts merely winched them forward — at a rate several times faster, however. Lumber companies extensively used these rugged, versatile craft on the Shield lakes of Ontario and Quebec. In the Muskoka watershed Alligators plied Lake of Bays, several lakes in the Oxtongue headwaters, and probably some others as well. You can see an Alligator,

THE STEAM ALLIGATOR. These strictly functional craft were a godsend to lumber companies who had to transport logs across the lakes that so frequently interrupted the Canadian Shield rivers. Two of the men in the photograph hold pike-poles, used for prodding and directing logs.   · Archives of Ontario S-5196

the *William M*, on display at the logging exhibit in Algon-quin Park. When log driving ended, many Alligators were simply abandoned on the shores of the lakes they last oper-ated on. A few derelicts can still be found in more remote regions.

While lumbering dams regulated water flows for the log drives, and steam tugs and Alligators made the lakes less of an obstacle, the actual channels of creeks and rivers often required improvements to permit the unimpeded flow of logs. Side dams or glance piers were frequently constructed, especially at falls and rapids, to keep logs from straying into secondary channels or onto shoals, where they might jam; booms also served that purpose. Obstructing rock outcrops and ledges were often blasted out to create a clear channel. Evidence of such blasting is visible at many Muskoka River waterfalls, where you will often also see imbedded in the rock iron bars that anchored piers, boom chains and other works. On the smaller creeks, lumber companies would brush out the dense choke of alders along the shores and remove deadheads and boulders from the channels in an effort to make them more drivable.

None of these improvements, however, could remedy the costly destruction of logs at many major waterfalls, or the total impossibility of sending logs over steep, rocky cascades on smaller streams. In these instances there was only one practical solution: construct log slides to by-pass the natural channel completely. Scores of log slides were built in the Muskoka watershed. The largest ran for hundreds of metres and ranked among the most impressive engineering works ever undertaken on the river.

A Muskoka River log slide typically consisted of an open trough constructed of thick planks and supported on crib-work or trestles. It started at a dam at the top of the water-fall and angled down over the adjacent slopes to safer waters below. A sluice in the dam admitted water and logs to the slide. Riding that cushion of water, the logs sped down the incline, flew off the end of the slide and plunged into the river. By all accounts the sights and sounds of one of the major slides in operation was nothing short of awesome.

In the 1860s and 1870s lumber companies often complained about the lack of slides on the Muskoka River. The imposing and violent South Falls on the South Muskoka stood out par-ticularly in this regard. At least one company blamed this cat-aract for holding up the eastward expansion of lumbering in Muskoka. Not surprisingly, the first major project undertaken by the Department of Public Works when it began making log-driving improvements on the Muskoka River after 1875 was a slide at South Falls. Started in 1878 and completed the following spring, this slide was 305 metres (1,000 feet) long, dropped 30.5 metres (100 feet) and could handle 600 logs per hour.

Shortly afterwards the Department of Public Works built another slide, this one by-passing Go Home Chute on the Go Home River (an alternate outlet to Georgian Bay from the Musquash River). In the early 1880s the Muskoka Slide, Dam and Boom Company built slides at Bracebridge Falls (240 metres, or 787 feet long) and Wilson's Falls on the North Muskoka, Campbell Falls on the Buck, and Sandy Gray's Chute on the Musquash. Other important slides in the west-ern part of the watershed included ones at High Falls (North Muskoka), Rosseau Falls (Rosseau River) and Clark Falls (Dee River).

SOUTH FALLS LOG SLIDE, 1907. *The busiest log slide in the Muskoka River system ran down the south wall of the South Falls chasm. In six decades of operation it carried millions of logs safely past the treacherous chutes.*

· National Archives Canada PA-56055

BRACEBRIDGE FALLS LOG SLIDE, *c. 1890.* This big slide started from a dam under the bridge at the top of the falls. Booms on the river above funneled logs into the sluiceway. Logs that have already negotiated the slide can be seen in the plunge pool below. This photograph also shows the Bird Woollen Mill as it looked after a modest expansion in 1888.

· Archives of Ontario Acc. 15963-16

LOG SLIDE UNDER CONSTRUCTION. In 1896 J.W. McNeice built this 90-metre-long (295-foot) slide for the Mickle Dyment Lumber Company of Gravenhurst. Running from Ragged Lake down into Smoke Lake, in the headwaters of the Oxtongue, it circumvented a steep, rocky creek channel. · Algonquin Park Museum #288 · W.S. McNeice

As logging operations moved eastward, a major slide was erected on the Hollow River near Dorset (this one 210 metres, or 689 feet long), and in 1893 the Gilmour Company built slides at Ragged Falls and High Falls on the Oxtongue. In the Oxtongue headwaters the Mickle Dyment Company constructed a slide between Ragged and Smoke lakes in 1896. Around 1900 the J.D. Shier Lumber Company built an even more impressive one between Big Porcupine and Ragged lakes. The Porcupine slide ran for 584 metres (1,914 feet) and dropped over 40 metres (131 feet).

The longest slide in the Muskoka watershed wasn't designed to carry logs past a waterfall. Rather, it formed an important link in what became known as the Gilmour Tramway, an ingenious scheme that carried logs *out* of the Muskoka River system. As mentioned earlier, the Gilmours had to transport their logs from the headwaters of the Oxtongue River (where they began logging in 1893) to their mills at the mouth of the Trent. The Oxtongue River and Lake of Bays made up the first leg of the route they chose. Then things got interesting.

Near Dorset, Lake of Bays is separated from St. Nora Lake (in the headwaters of the Gull-Trent River) by only ten kilometres (6 miles), with Raven Lake at the head of the Black River sandwiched in between. By erecting strategically placed lumbering dams, the Gilmours could drive their logs from the Black River, just below Raven Lake, down a marshy valley to St. Nora. But how could they first transport millions of feet of logs overland and raise them more than 35 metres (115 feet) in the process, from Lake of Bays to Raven Lake?

The answer: the Tramway. Here's what the Gilmours did. On the south shore of Lake of Bays, just west of Dorset, they constructed a jackladder (chained conveyor) at least 30 metres

RAGGED FALLS LOG SLIDE, *Oxtongue River. It was preferable to build log slides in a straight line, but the local physiography forced the Gilmour Company to construct a curving trough here in 1893. The lower portion (not visible) did run straight down to the foot of the falls. This old postcard incorrectly identifies the falls.*

· Algonquin Park Museum #3860 · Swan

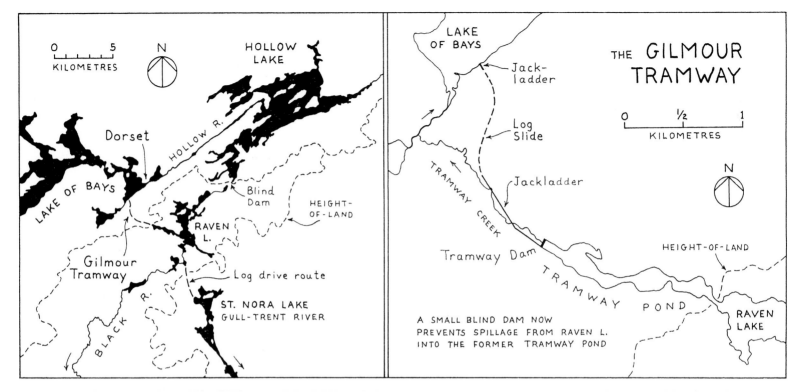

INTERESTING JUXTAPOSITION OF RIVER SYSTEMS and convenient gaps in the heights of land near Dorset spawned bold lumbermen's schemes in the late 1800s. Using Raven Lake on the Black River as a stepping-stone, the Gilmours vaulted their logs from Lake of Bays on the Muskoka River to St. Nora Lake in the headwaters of the Gull - Trent.

The Gilmours weren't the only lumbermen who faced the problem of logs on the Muskoka but mills on the Trent. More than a decade before they set their ingenious tramway in motion, Mossom Boyd wanted to drive logs from Hollow Lake to his mills at Bobcaygeon (in the Kawartha Lakes reach of the Trent system).

Boyd proposed to divert water, and logs, from Hollow Lake to Raven Lake along a short valley cutting through the height of land (a blind dam, near one built by lumbermen in the 1880s, prevents Hollow Lake from escaping in that direction today). He would then divert the logs from the Black River to St. Nora Lake in the same way that the Gilmours eventually did.

Unfortunately for Boyd, Muskoka River lumber firms vigorously opposed the scheme, fearing the loss of water from the Muskoka system would jeopardize their own drives. The Ontario government turned thumbs down on Boyd in 1882.

(100 feet) long which lifted the logs some 12 metres (43 feet) up a hillside. A steam engine in an adjacent stone power-house operated the jackladder and also pumped water up the hill. At the top the logs and water entered a log slide. This impressive structure ran about 1,000 metres (3,280 feet) cross-country, dropping only a few metres, to the entrance of a narrow creek valley or pass that ascended between high hills to Raven Lake. At the end of the slide a second jackladder took over. Climbing about 27 metres (89 feet) over a distance of nearly 800 metres (2,625 feet), it lifted the logs to the top of a stone dam, the Tramway Dam, further up the pass. Water from this dam spun a turbine that operated the jackladder.

The Tramway Dam created an artificial waterway called the Tramway Pond. It flooded the pass 1.7 kilometres (1 mile) right over to Raven Lake, which was raised to help effect the connection. The Gilmours used an Alligator to warp booms of logs along the Tramway Pond from the dam and then down Raven Lake to the Black River.

The Tramway was a huge undertaking. It took a year just to saw out all the lumber needed, and another year to build it. The cost was over a million dollars. Although the Tram-way and the connecting links to St. Nora Lake worked, the system proved an inefficient method of moving logs. It took two seasons to put all the logs, driven down to Lake of Bays in 1895, over the heights of land. Not surprisingly the Gil-mours abandoned the Tramway after the 1896 season in favour of their new Canoe Lake sawmill.

GILMOUR JACKLADDER, *Tramway Creek, c. 1895. From the end of the log slide (visible in the background), the logs travelled up this water-powered jackladder to the Tramway Dam and Pond.* · Algonquin Park Museum #1097
· Ministry of Natural Resources

GILMOUR POWERHOUSE AND JACKLADDER, *Lake of Bays, c. 1895. Logs began their journey over the Gilmour Tramway at this jackladder, which raised them up a hillside from the lake and then dumped them in a log slide. Water for the slide was pumped up through the large pipes in the foreground.*

· National Archives Canada C-21212

GILMOUR TRAMWAY LOG SLIDE. *This impressive slide carried logs 1,000 metres (3,280 feet) cross-country from the top of the Lake of Bays jackladder to the base of a second jackladder.*

GILMOUR ALLIGATOR ON TRAMWAY POND, *c. 1895.* *The Gilmours used a steam Alligator to* *warp booms of logs down this artificial waterway to Raven Lake and thence to the Black River outlet. Water and* *logs from the Black were then diverted three kilometres (2 miles) over into St. Nora Lake, in the headwaters of the* *Gull · Trent River system.*   · Algonquin Park Museum #1095 · Ministry of Natural Resources

Today, some evidence of the Gilmour Tramway still exists, most notably the stone powerhouse on Lake of Bays (now a private cottage) and the Tramway Dam. The latter is overgrown and cut through so that the Tramway Pond is just a series of beaver ponds and marshes. The jackladders and slide themselves are gone. Indeed, none of the dozens of great log slides that served Muskoka River lumbermen have survived intact. At a few waterfalls you can still trace the old slide routes by low railway-like embankments, rock cuts, rotting timbers and iron anchoring bars in the rock. Notable examples include the South Falls, Hollow River and Ragged Lake slides.

Log drives on the Muskoka River traditionally took place in the spring, or at least began then, to take advantage of the abundant waters of the freshet. In that era lumber companies conducted their logging operations in the winter. They used horse-drawn sleighs to transport the logs to the nearest drivable stream or a lake drained by one. They piled the logs up on the shores of the streams or right out on the ice of the lake to await the spring break-up and the long journey down to the mills.

Once the drive got under way, the river drivers maintained a constant vigil for trouble. Leaping from log to log or wading in the frigid swirling waters, they used their pike-poles and peaveys (modified cant-hooks) to prod and pry the heavy logs away from snags, shoals, back eddies and secondary channels — keep it moving, that was the name of the game. What they feared most was a jam. Jams happened often and if they weren't quickly broken the current relentlessly piled the logs up into huge river-blocking masses.

The dangerous heart-in-mouth task of releasing big jams fell to volunteer "jam-crackers." Balanced precariously on slippery rocks and logs or suspended by ropes in narrow chasms they carefully removed logs at the base of the jam until they located the key log, the one holding the whole thing back. Sometimes it was necessary to winch logs out, or if all else failed, blast the jam. When a jam went, it usually went suddenly and the river drivers had to be fleet-footed indeed to reach shore safely. Many didn't make it. Injury and death were the grim realities of driving logs.

The river drivers' jobs involved more than just preventing or breaking up jams. At dams and slides they had to direct the logs into the sluiceways (semi-permanent camps were maintained at major dams and slides). Every time the drive entered a lake they had to gather the logs into booms for towing, and after the main body of logs passed down a river, "sweepers" tailed along behind to manoeuvre into the current all the logs that had become stranded in backwaters or shallows.

For transportation down the rivers the drivers employed a variety of boats, depending on the nature of the particular stream. The classic, perhaps, was the pointer, developed in the 1850s in the Ottawa Valley for J.R. Booth. A shallow-draught wooden skiff with characteristically pointed bow and stern, it was highly manoeuvrable and ideal for use on fast-flowing rivers filled with logs and rapids. Pointers saw some use on the Hollow and Oxtongue rivers, if not elsewhere in the Muskoka watershed.

Because the logs of the various lumber companies got intermixed during the drives, each firm stamped its logs with a special hammer face bearing the company mark. The logs were sorted out at a sorting jack at the end of the drive. Before the practice of marking the logs began, and before lumber companies began to co-operate in the improvement of rivers and the operation of drives, springtime was often a rather wild time as each company fought to get its logs downriver first when there was lots of water. Of course things got pretty wild anyway when the drive went through or near a settlement and men, unable to resist temptation after a winter in isolated lumber camps, drank and brawled their way through local taverns.

Log drives on the Muskoka River frequently went on right into the summer on the larger streams. As a result friction often developed between lumber companies and navigation interests when logs impeded waterways used by steamboats. This problem particularly affected the Muskoka River below Bracebridge, where some lumber companies, notably Mickle Dyment, liked to let unboomed logs drift down to Lake Muskoka. Some of the disputes ended up in the courts. At the sawmills the lumber companies simply stored the logs in the adjacent river or lake until they could be stockpiled on shore or sawn. Muskoka Bay at Gravenhurst was often so choked with logs that it was claimed, probably without much exaggeration, that you could walk right across it without getting your feet wet.

Over the years many different activities have depended on the Muskoka River system — navigation, water-powered mills, hydroelectric development, recreation and tourism — but none have utilized the lakes and streams to the extent that log driving did, or affected them in so many ways. All the way from the Algonquin Highland to Georgian Bay, along the smallest creeks and the largest rivers, practically every part of the Muskoka River system served as a water highway for the lumbermen.

We're fortunate that many of the stories, artifacts and photographs of the log-driving era in Ontario have been preserved in books, museums and archives. In the bibliography of this book you'll find references for a few books and articles that include accounts of log driving in the Muskoka watershed. You might also want to visit the Woodmere Logging Museum, owned and operated by Jim and Marty Wood right here in Muskoka. Located on Highway 117 between Bracebridge and Baysville, it boasts an excellent collection of lumbering artifacts, including a pointer boat. And of course the Alligator *William* M is a focal point of the pioneer logging exhibit in Algonquin Park (located just off Highway 60 near the East Gate).

The log-driving era, the steamboat era, the water-mill era, and all the other interesting chapters in the story of the Muskoka River — it is important that we don't forget any of these vital components of local history. If you had not realized it before, then perhaps you do now: the natural and cultural heritage of Muskoka owes its richness and diversity in large measure to the influences of the river — This River the Muskoka.

DOWN THE RIVER. *On large, placid rivers the logs floated easily in the current (the river drivers would have to sweep out any timber hung up along the shores). Here, on the Muskoka River below Bracebridge, the steamer Islander has to contend with this perennial navigation hazard.* · National Archives Canada PA-32260

READY TO GO. *Each spring the upper lakes filled up with logs awaiting the long drive down the rivers to the sawmills. These logs on Buck Lake probably faced a relatively short journey to mills in Huntsville.* · Archives of Ontario Acc. 2203-S-3667

ALLIGATOR AND POINTERS *on Burntroot Lake, Algonquin Park, 1908. Although this scene is just across the height of land in the headwaters of the Petawawa River, you would have witnessed much the same activity and landscape on the nearby headwater lakes of the Muskoka River system during the log-driving era.*

· Algonquin Park Museum #3005 · University of Toronto

OUT OF THE HILLS! Aided by dams and slides the drive crews wrestled the big pine logs down scores of small streams to the main rivers. This scene is along an unidentified creek in the Muskoka watershed.

· Archives of Ontario Acc. 2203·S·3625

166

LOG JAM! — *the river drivers' worst nightmare. This jam developed at Sandy Gray's Chute on the Musquash River in 1939, near the end of the log-driving era in the Muskoka River system.*　　·Ontario Hydro

END OF THE JOURNEY — ALMOST. *Pine logs carpet Muskoka Bay at Gravenhurst. Screaming saws in one of the big steam-powered mills (such as that of the Rathbun Company in this photograph) will slice through them. Trains will whisk the resulting lumber away to Canadian and American markets to the south.*

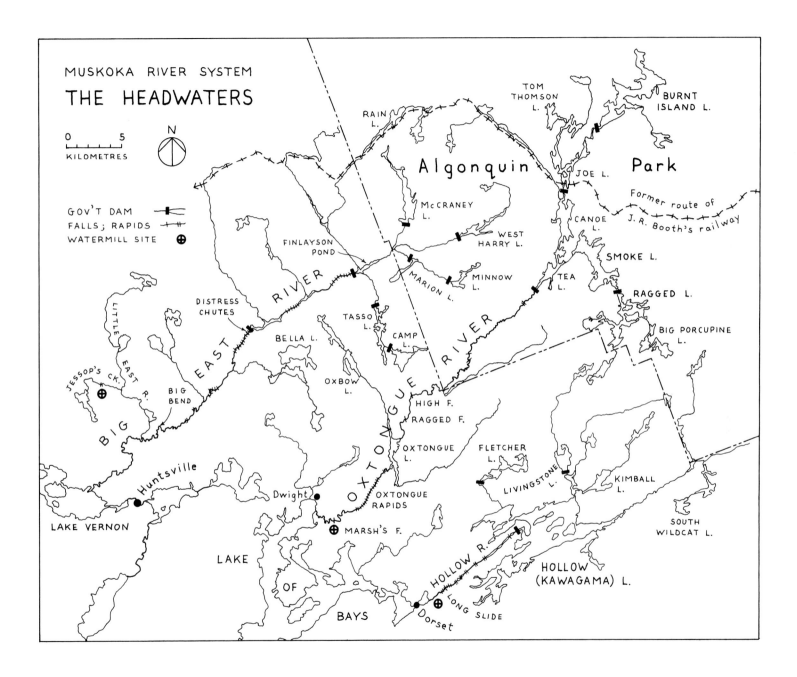

MUSKOKA RIVER SYSTEM
THE HEADWATERS

0   5

KILOMETRES

N

GOV'T DAM

FALLS; RAPIDS

WATERMILL SITE

RAIN L.

TOM THOMSON L.

BURNT ISLAND L.

Algonquin   Park

McCRANEY L.

JOE L.

Former route of J.R. Booth's railway

CANOE L.

WEST HARRY L.

SMOKE L.

FINLAYSON POND

MARION L.

MINNOW L.

TEA L.

RAGGED L.

DISTRESS CHUTES

EAST RIVER

TASSO L.

CAMP L.

BIG PORCUPINE L.

BELLA L.

OXBOW L.

OXTONGUE RIVER

JESSOP'S CK.

BIG BEND

LITTLE EAST R.

BIG

HIGH F.

RAGGED F.

FLETCHER L.

Huntsville

OXTONGUE L.

KIMBALL L.

Dwight

OXTONGUE

LIVINGSTONE L.

LAKE VERNON

OXTONGUE RAPIDS

SOUTH WILDCAT L.

MARSH'S F.

LAKE

HOLLOW R.

HOLLOW (KAWAGAMA) L.

OF

LONG SLIDE

BAYS

Dorset

169

BUCK LAKE

AXE L.

AXE CK.

BUCK R.

FOX L.

HOODSTOWN R.

BLACK CK.

Ravenscliffe

BALLANTINE'S CK.

WALKER L.

The Canal

FAIRY L.

PENINSULA LAKE

Dwight

LAKE VERNON

Huntsville

RIVER

Huntsville Lock

Route of Portage Railway

LAKE OF BAYS

MUSKOKA RIVER SYSTEM

THE **NORTH** AND **SOUTH** **MUSKOKA**

MARY LAKE

Port Sydney

PORT SYDNEY F.

CLEARWATER L.

DEVINE L.

BIGWIN ISLAND

Dorset

ECHO L.

0   5
KILOMETRES

BALSAM CHUTE

N

Baysville

DUCK CHUTE

NORTH MUSKOKA

SOUTH MUSKOKA RIVER

SLATER'S CHUTE

▲ HIGH FALLS

LEGEND

GOVERNMENT DAM

WATERFALLS

WATERMILL SITE ⊕

HYDROELECTRIC STATION

OPERATING ▲

FORMER △

⊕▲ WILSON'S F.

⊕ HALSTEAD'S R.

Bracebridge

⊕△ BRACEBRIDGE
▲ FALLS

CROZIER'S R.

WOOD L.

LAKE MUSKOKA

SOUTH FALLS ▲

▲ MATTHIAS FALLS

⊕▲

HANNA CHUTE

⊕▲ TRETHEWEY FALLS

Gravenhurst

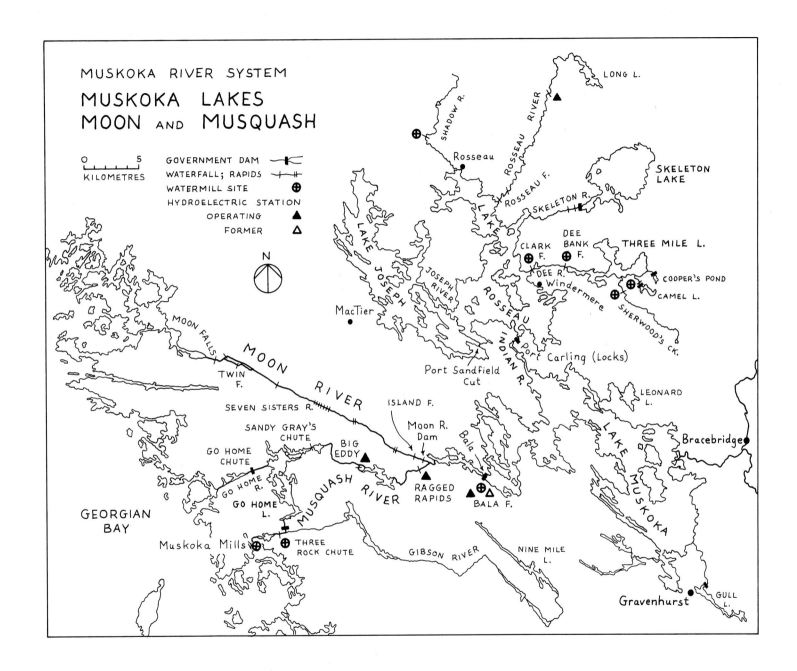

MUSKOKA RIVER SYSTEM

MUSKOKA LAKES
MOON AND MUSQUASH

0 ____ 5
KILOMETRES

GOVERNMENT DAM
WATERFALL; RAPIDS
WATERMILL SITE ⊕
HYDROELECTRIC STATION
OPERATING ▲
FORMER △

N

LONG L.

SHADOW R.

ROSSEAU RIVER ▲

Rosseau

ROSSEAU F.

SKELETON R.

SKELETON LAKE

LAKE ROSSEAU

DEE BANK

CLARK F. ⊕   DEE BANK F. ⊕

THREE MILE L.

DEE R.

Windermere

COOPER'S POND

CAMEL L.

SHERWOOD'S CK.

LAKE JOSEPH

JOSEPH RIVER

MacTier

INDIAN R.

Port Carling (Locks)

Port Sandfield
Cut

MOON FALLS

MOON RIVER

TWIN F.

SEVEN SISTERS R.

SANDY GRAY'S CHUTE

GO HOME CHUTE

BIG EDDY ▲

ISLAND F.

Moon R. Dam

RAGGED RAPIDS ▲

Bala

⊕ ▲ △

BALA F.

LEONARD L.

Bracebridge

LAKE MUSKOKA

GEORGIAN BAY

GO HOME R.

GO HOME L.

MUSQUASH RIVER

Muskoka Mills ⊕

THREE ROCK CHUTE ⊕

GIBSON RIVER

NINE MILE L.

GULL L.

Gravenhurst

BIBLIOGRAPHY

Significant subject matter dealing with the Muskoka River is noted after each entry when not obvious from the title.

HISTORIES AND DESCRIPTIONS

Addison, Ottelyn. *Early Days in Algonquin Park*. Toronto: McGraw-Hill Ryerson Ltd., 1974. (Gilmour Drive, resort hotels in Oxtongue headwaters)

Avery, Sidney G. *Reflections: Muskoka and Lake of Bays of Yesteryear*. Bracebridge: Herald-Gazette Press, 1974. (Hollow River log drives, Gilmour Tramway)

Bice, Ralph. *Along the Trail with Ralph Bice in Algonquin Park*. Toronto: Consolidated Amethyst Communications Inc., 1980. (Gilmour Drive)

Boyer, Barbaranne. *Muskoka's Grand Hotels*. Erin: The Boston Mills Press, 1987.

Boyer, Robert J. *A Good Town Grew Here: The Story of Bracebridge, Ontario*. Bracebridge: Herald-Gazette Press, 1975. (early mills and hydro development at Bracebridge Falls)

———. *Early Exploration and Surveying of Muskoka District*. Bracebridge: Herald-Gazette Press, 1979.

———. *Woodchester Villa*. Bracebridge: Bracebridge Historical Society, 1982. (Henry Bird and the Bird Woollen Mill)

Bragg, Roger. "Muskoka Wood Manufacturing." *East Georgian Bay Historical Journal*, Vol. 2, 93-123. Elmvale: East Georgian Bay Historical Foundation, 1982. (Muskoka Wood log drives, Big East and Buck rivers)

Brown, Ron. *Ghost Towns of Ontario, Vol. 1*. Toronto: Cannonbooks, 1978. (Muskoka Mills)

Cookson, Joe. *Tattle Tales of Muskoka*. Bracebridge: Herald-Gazette Press, 1976. (Big East River log drives, early resorts on Fairy and Peninsula lakes)

———. *Roots in Muskoka*. Bracebridge: Herald-Gazette Press, 1978. (Ballantine's grist mill)

Coombe, Geraldine. *Muskoka Past and Present*. Toronto: McGraw-Hill Ryerson Ltd., 1976. (Sandy Gray, Walker's Mill, Baysville)

Cope, Leila M. *A History of the Village of Port Carling*. Bracebridge: Herald-Gazette Press, 1956.

Demaine, Marjorie, ed. *Stories of Early Muskoka Days — Memoirs of W.H. Demaine*. Bracebridge: Herald-Gazette Press, 1971. (Hoodstown, Black Creek mills)

———. *Chronicles of Stisted Township*. Bracebridge: Herald-Gazette Press, 1976. (Hoodstown, Axe Creek log drives, Howell's mill)

Devitt, Ed H., and Nila Reynolds. *Echoes of the Past, Resounding in the Present*. n.d. (a history of the Dorset-North Haliburton area, including the Gilmour Tramway)

Dickson, James. *Camping in the Muskoka Region*. Toronto: Ontario Department of Lands and Forests, 1959. Originally published 1886. (canoe trip up the Oxtongue River)

Findlay, Mary Lynn. *Lures and Legends of Lake of Bays*. Bracebridge: Herald-Gazette Press, 1973. (mills at Baysville, Shrigley's mill)

Guillet, Edwin C. *Early Life in Upper Canada*. Toronto: The Ontario Publishing Company, 1933. (overview of grist-milling, lumbering and sawmilling in what is now Ontario)

Hamilton, W.E., John Rogers and Seymour Penson. *Guide Book and Atlas of Muskoka and Parry Sound Districts*. Toronto: H.R. Page and Co., 1879. (scenic description, local history, water-mill locations on maps)

Johnson, George H. *Port Sydney Past*. Erin: The Boston Mills Press, 1980. (mills at Port Sydney Falls)

Kirkwood, Alexander, and J.J. Murphy, eds. *The Undeveloped Lands in Northern and Western Ontario*. Toronto: Hunter, Rose and Co., 1878. (Muskoka River water power, Bracebridge-area water mills)

MacKay, Donald. *The Lumberjacks*. Toronto: McGraw-Hill Ryerson Ltd., 1978. (colourful account of early Canadian lumbering; see esp. Chapter 8, The River Drivers)

MacKay, Niall. *By Steam Boat and Steam Train, The Story of the Huntsville and Lake of Bays Railway and Navigation Companies*. Erin: The Boston Mills Press, 1982.

McEachern, Ruth, Kerry Greenaway and Susan McKay. *Dorset*. Bracebridge: Herald-Gazette Press, 1976. (Shrigley water mill)

Municipal Electric Commission Centennial Histories (1967) for Bracebridge, Gravenhurst, Huntsville, and Orillia.

Murray, Florence B., ed. *Muskoka and Haliburton, 1615-1875: A Collection of Documents*. Toronto: University of Toronto Press, 1963. (early exploration, surveying, lumbering, etc. in Muskoka watershed)

Reynolds, John. *Windmills and Watermills*. New York: Praeger Publishers, 1970. (history of world water-mill development)

Saunders, Audrey. *Algonquin Story*. Toronto: Ontario Department of Lands and Forests, 1947. (establishment of Algonquin Park; Gilmour Drive; Ragged and Big Porcupine Lake log slides)

Shea, William Albert. *History of the Sheas and Birth of a Township*. n.d. (water mills in the Dee River basin)

Smith, Gail. "Bird's Woollen Mill," *An Introduction to the History of Muskoka*, Section B. Muskoka Board of Education, 1975.

Tatley, Richard. *The Steamboat Era in the Muskokas, Vol. 1: To the Golden Years*. Erin: The Boston Mills Press, 1983.

————. *The Steamboat Era in the Muskokas, Vol. 2: The Golden Years to Present*. Erin: The Boston Mills Press, 1984.

Thomas, Redmond. *Reminiscences (Bracebridge, Muskoka)*. Bracebridge: Herald-Gazette Press, 1969. (Bracebridge Falls grist mill, Norwood Mills)

Tozer, Ron, and Dan Strickland. A *Pictorial History of Algonquin Provincial Park*. Ministry of Natural Resources, 1980. (lumbering, log drives, tourism)

Wood, Marty. "Lumbering in Muskoka." *Muskoka Sun* (1979). (log drives)

TECHNICAL BOOKS AND REPORTS

Atmospheric Environment Service. *Temperature and Precipitation, Ontario, 1941-1970*. Ottawa: Environment Canada, 1972.

Beak Consultants Ltd. *Environmental Assessment of Potential Hydro-electric Developments on the Lower Musquash River* (1979). (prepared for the Orillia Water, Light and Power Commission)

Beatty, F.W. *List of Water Powers in the Province of Ontario*. Toronto: Department of Lands and Forests, 1946. (waterfall and water-mill data)

Bureau of Forestry (Ontario). Replies to questionnaire of January 15, 1897, re sawmills and timber cut on private land. (water-mill data)

Census of Canada, 1871. Schedule 6, Return of Industrial Establishments (water-mill statistics, Muskoka)

Chapman, L.J., and D.F. Putnam. *The Physiography of Southern Ontario*, 3rd edition. Toronto: Ministry of Natural Resources, 1984. (glacial recession and Lake Algonquin)

Denis, Leo G., and Arthur V. White. *Water-Powers of Canada*. Ottawa: Commission of Conservation, 1911. (waterfall, water-mill and hydroelectric data)

Denis, Leo G. *Electric Generation and Distribution in Canada*. Ottawa: Commission of Conservation, 1918. (details of Muskoka River hydroelectric stations)

Douglas, R.J.W. (scientific editor). *Geology and Economic Minerals of Canada*, 5th edition. Ottawa: Geological Survey of Canada, 1976. (glacial and post-glacial events affecting Muskoka watershed)

Electrical News and Engineering. Toronto, 1891-1950. (hydroelectric development, Muskoka River)

Guillet, G.R. *Geological Guide to Highway 60, Algonquin Provincial Park*, M.P. 29. Toronto: Ontario Department of Mines, 1969. (bedrock geology, Smoke Lake)

Hewitt, D.F. *Geology and Mineral Deposits of the Parry Sound-Huntsville Area*, Geological Report 52. Toronto: Ontario Department of Mines, 1967. (geology of western part of Muskoka watershed)

Hough, Jack L. *Geology of the Great Lakes*. Urbana: University of Illinois Press, 1958. (Lake Algonquin events)

MacLaren Plansearch (consultant). *Muskoka River System — Water Management Improvement Study, Recommendations* (1984). (prepared for Environment Canada and Ontario Ministry of Natural Resources)

McNeice, L.G. (engineer, Orillia Water, Light and Power Commission). "Matthias Falls Power Development on South Branch of Muskoka River." *Electrical News and Engineering*, Vol. 59, No. 10, 1950, 38-41.

Ontario Department of Lands and Forests. *Sawmill Licentiate Book, 1924-30*. (licensed watermills on Muskoka River with capacity)

Ontario Hydro. *Annual Report*, 1908-1964. (details of hydroelectric developments on Muskoka River)

————. *Statistical Yearbook*, 1971-1980.

Ontario Ministry of Natural Resources. *Water Level Regulation in Muskoka* (1977).

————. "Skeleton Lake Meteor Crater Proposal." *Earth Science Inventory Checklist* (1979).

————. Unpublished water resources data — lakes, rivers, dams, etc. in the Muskoka watershed.

Phillips, D.W., and J.A.W. McCulloch. *The Climate of the Great Lakes Basin*. Toronto: Atmospheric Environment Service, Environment Canada, 1972. (climate and weather data on Algonquin Dome)

"Report of the Commissioner of Public Works." *Ontario Sessional Papers*. Toronto, 1868-1956. (government dams, locks and log slides in Muskoka watershed)

Roger, Alexander. *Central Electric Stations in Canada, Part II — Directory* (May 1, 1928), Water Resources Paper 55. Ottawa: Department of the Interior, 1929. (statistics of Muskoka River hydro stations)

Rorke, L.V. *List of Water Powers in the Province of Ontario*. Toronto: Department of Lands and Forests, 1925. (waterfalls and water-mill data)

Sharpe, D.R. "Quaternary Geology of the Gravenhurst, Bracebridge and Huntsville Areas, District Municipality of Muskoka,

koka." *Summary of Field Work, 1978, by the Ontario Geological Survey* (M.P. 82), 152-54. (glacial deposits, Lake Algonquin)

Shawinigan Energy Consultants Ltd. *Feasibility Study, New Generating Facilities on the Lower Musquash River* (1978). (prepared for the Orillia Water, Light and Power Commission)

Statistics Canada. *Electric Power Statistics, Vol. III, Inventory of Prime Mover and Electric Generating Equipment* (1971-). (hydroelectric station data)

Water Survey of Canada. *Historical Streamflow Summary, Ontario, to 1986.* Ottawa: Environment Canada, 1987. (mean monthly and annual flows, and extremes of discharge, for Muskoka River gauging stations)

White, James. *Altitudes in the Dominion of Canada,* 2nd edition. Ottawa: Commission of Conservation, 1915. (waterfall heights and elevations, Muskoka River)

NEWSPAPERS

Bracebridge *Herald-Gazette*
Bracebridge *Gazette*
Huntsville *Forester*
Muskoka Herald (Bracebridge)
Muskoka Sun (Bracebridge)

REGISTRY OFFICE, Muskoka (Bracebridge)

Abstract books for selected townships and villages, and various plans and instruments listed in them (water-mill ownership and location)

MAPS AND AERIAL PHOTOGRAPHS

National Topographic Maps (1:50,000 scale) — Department of Energy, Mines and Resources, Ottawa.

Ontario Basic Mapping (1:10,000 scale) — Ontario Ministry of Natural Resources, Toronto.

Aerial photographs (1:15,840 scale) — Ontario Ministry of Natural Resources, Toronto.

I would especially like to thank Mr. Wayne Corry, water control supervisor with the Ministry of Natural Resources in Huntsville, for cheerfully providing an abundance of information. In addition, the following individuals supplied useful information not available in public sources: Mrs. Reta Bogart (Ufford); Mr. John Fiorini (Shannon Hall); Mr. George H. Johnson (Port Sydney/Port Credit); Mr. Bruce Keown (Oxtongue Lake); Mr. Frank Near (Toronto); Mr. Ian Shepherd (Baysville); Mr. Dave Shea (Ufford); Mr. Joe Stocking (Huntsville); and Mr. Jim Wood (Woodmere Logging Museum, near Baysville).